The Awakening of Man

Godavari Parulekar

A translation of the
Sahitya Akademi Award winning book
Jevha Manus Jaga Hoto

Translated by
Nikhil Gavankar

Popular Prakashan
www.popularprakashan.com

Published by Harsha Bhatkal
for Popular Prakashan Pvt. Ltd.
301, Mahalaxmi Chambers
22, Bhulabhai Desai Road
Mumbai 400026
www.popularprakashan.com

First Published 2015

(4418)
ISBN: 978-81-7991-859-3

Cover: Dattatraya Padekar
Design: Mahendra Ghanekar
Typesetting: Anjali Sawant

Printed by
Repro Knowledgecast Limited
Building No A1,GEBI Industrial Park
OPP. Reliance Petrol Pump
Village Sonale, Thane - 421302

Contents

Introduction by Late Comrade Govind Pansare

India has a long tradition of dedicated, idealistic, selfless social and political workers. It is important to read about and understand this tradition and to acknowledge that the Communist Party has contributed immensely to this tradition.

Comrade Godavari Parulekar reached great heights in the Communist Party, like other outstanding women workers, due to her accomplishments and untiring efforts. The educated reader in India does not know of her tireless contributions for certain reasons. Communists have generally hesitated to speak about their work and activities which, to me, is a major flaw. Very little has been written about the history of the social struggles in the country in which so many Communist leaders have participated. This history would be a great repository of learning for society in general.

When I was asked to write a few words about *Godutai*, I became keenly aware of this lacuna. Apart from *Godutai's* Marathi book *Jevha Manus Jaga Hoto* and a short article by Comrade Ashok Dhawale, there is very little literature available on the activities of *Godutai* and Shamrao Parulekar. The regional literature of the Warli tribe has innumerable references to *Godutai* Parulekar, and any mention of the Warli uprising has to start and end with *Godutai* Parulekar irrespective of the ideological leanings of the writer.

Godutai was born Godavari Gokhale and was the daughter of a prominent and well-to-do lawyer in Pune Laxman Rao Gokhale, who was a member of the moderate faction of the Congress Party, a freedom fighter, and cousin to the freedom fighter and thinker Gopal Krishna Gokhale.

Godutai was educated in Pune and completed her masters in economics and political science and then studied for the Bar exam to train as a lawyer. She was the first woman lawyer from Maharashtra. Among her colleagues were distinguished persons such as SM Joshi, NG Gore and Achyutrao Patwardhan.

Her family status rendered her 'upper class' and 'upper caste', but she spent a major part of her life with *Adivasis* and directed and participated in their struggle. It is often argued that a person from the 'upper class' and 'upper caste' can never understand the problems and suffering of the lowest strata of society. But *Godutai* and her husband Shamrao Parulekar proved this wrong through their deeds over a period of more than five decades. She was a classic example exposing the limitations of a theoretically argued philosophical position.

Godutai plunged into the Indian freedom struggle at a very young age and had to face imprisonment immediately. Her father was also an opponent of British rule, but his political views were moderate. He was displeased with the fact that *Godutai* was imprisoned and reproached her in harsh terms about her political activities. He decided to break all relations with her and a very despondent *Godutai* had to leave Pune and go to Mumbai. There she joined an organisation called The Servants Society of India. She was the first woman member of this society.

The Servants Society of India was moderate in its political stance, which did not match the outlook of *Godutai* and Shamrao. They soon left the organisation to become members of the Communist Party where they remained until their deaths. The major part of their life's work was among the *Adivasis* of the Warli tribe near Mumbai.

Godutai and Shamrao Parulekar

Godutai and Shamrao Parulekar were married on May 24, 1939 after many years of social and political activities together. Shamrao suffered a stroke in 1964 when he was in Arthur Road jail and died. *Godutai* was with him in jail when he died.

Shamrao and *Godutai* had immense love and respect for each other. In 1962, *Godutai*, Shamrao, and many prominent Communist leaders were lodged in different jails across the country. I was also imprisoned during those days. I was very young then and the time I spent in jail with these veteran Communist leaders proved invaluable in shaping my political and social outlook. I had cleared the Bar exam and was a lawyer attached to Yerawada jail in Pune.

Comrade BT Ranadive, Comrade Bardhan, Comrade Madhav Rao Gaekwad, Comrade Chandragupta Choudhary, Comrade Rangnekar, and many others were in jail together. *Godutai*, Ahilya Rangnekar, and Karuna Choudhary were among the female prisoners. We would meet whenever we had to file a habeas corpus petition in the High Court or the Supreme Court of India. These meetings and discussions are a treasured memory.

Comrade Ranadive would often make a remark regarding Shamrao Parulekar. BT Ranadive was known to be a hardliner among Communists. He had a sharp and incisive mind with a good sense of humour. Shamrao was addicted to smoking cigarettes, and as one cigarette burned to the end, a new one would appear in its place. Ranadive would say that Shamrao started his day with a cigarette and ended it with a cigarette. I played bridge with Shamrao and BT Ranadive in jail. Although I never understood the game, they needed a partner.

Jevha Manus Jaga Hoto

Godutai's book of just 160 pages, first published in 1970, is a landmark in Marathi autobiographical literature. It was written with the inspiration and support of Shamrao Parulekar.

In the author's introductory note to the first edition, *Godutai* writes:

> *When Shri P Bhagwat insisted that I write the introductory note to the book, I would sit down to write it. But tears streamed from my eyes and I had to put the papers aside. The memories of my dear husband Comrade Shamrao would overwhelm me. My heart suffered the stab of separation and I felt I was being torn apart inside. I felt guilty for being alive.*

In November 1962, when we were in jail together Comrade Shamrao had said that I should write about my activities with the Adivasis. I was not sure that I was ready for the task. I was not a writer, and I generally did not enjoy writing. As a result, I never found the courage to start writing anything. I felt that nothing substantial would be achieved by writing about these activities and so I would put off the task on some silly excuse.

When Shamrao persisted, I finally relented, and in 1964, wrote two chapters called "Warli Life on the Fringes of Society" and "Our Homes". Shamrao was very happy with the drafts of these two chapters, and that made me feel satisfied. After that I did not find the time to write anything else.

Godutai was elected the president of the Bharatiya Kisan Sabha because of her selfless work and devotion to the party over such a long period of time. She was the first woman to reach the highest level of this or any similar national organisation of farmers.

It is impossible to cover the range and depth of Godavari Parulekar's activities among *Adivasis* and farmers in the constraints of an article, and that is not my intention. But it is necessary to state that the pinnacle of her achievements have been with the *Adivasis* and farmers in India.

Godavari Parulekar died on October 8, 1996, and I end this note with a quote from the address she delivered at the 15th convention of the Communist Party (Marxist): "I have reached the sunset of my life now, but I take satisfaction in the fact that I spent more than five decades of my life with the Communist Party and the Kisan Sabha fighting for the rights of the dispossessed against the might of national and international institutional forces."

— Late Comrade Govind Pansare

Introduction by Dr Subhashchandra Bhelke

Human beings strive for a happy and fulfilled life. Only a life lived with dignity makes happiness and fulfilment possible. The human life is not lived in isolation, especially a life of dignity, happiness, and fulfilment. Problems in the path of happiness and fulfilment appear when the social mechanism gives a privileged class the upper hand to seize the achievements of the society at large. Many are deprived of their legitimate dues in such a society. Instead, they are exploited at the hands of the privileged and suffer oppression and injustice. This is a human concern of stripping a person of dignity. The injustice enters social life when a group of people becomes wealthy and powerful.

The oppression is first economic and is then made stronger and sustainable by political oppression. This social reality, though undesirable, itself creates a pressure to change for the better and obtain dignified living conditions for the oppressed and exploited groups in society. Such a challenge takes the shape of an inevitable social alternative as a historical necessity which fructifies through a process that was identified and conceptually formulated by Karl Marx as dialectical materialism.

In modern times, this upsurge was informed by Marxist thought and propelled revolutionary activities in several places, especially where conditions for such an upsurge were ripe. This legacy, from the 19th century onwards, attached social changes to the prongs of economic and political theories. The moral sensitivity of contemplative minds impelled them to undertake the task of changing the destiny of the oppressed classes and begin movements for social uplift. An Indian chapter of this epic battle for human dignity is the life story of Godavari Parulekar and her husband Shamrao Parulekar.

Together they began a movement among the Warlis in the Adivasi region of Thane district in Maharashtra. They led the movement against oppression, exploitation, and slavery of *Adivasis*. As leaders, they built the character of a self-respecting Adivasi by giving them the confidence to fight their inhuman repression. The Parulekars did not instigate the community to violent or destructive activities. Theirs was a mature and moral leadership that gives direction so that the force is generated within the oppressed through the process of awakening their sense of dignity and justice.

The Parulekars mobilised the peasantry through the All India and Maharashtra Rajya Kisan Sabhas. As a part of the struggle, they spent some time in jail but without any regrets. Theirs was a life of commitment and sacrifice for a greater social cause. *Godavaritai* lived for a quarter century after the untimely demise of her husband. She made a unique contribution through her activities. She also made a noteworthy contribution to the world of literature through books about her activities and experiences of the movement. In spite of being a woman from a traditional background, she showed exceptional courage and rose above all limitations to lead social movements. She will be remembered by future generations for her vision, dedication, selfless efforts, and relentless struggle to free the oppressed class from its inhuman conditions of slavery.

— Dr Subhashchandra Bhelke
Professor, Department of Philosophy
University of Pune

Short Introduction by the Translator

Every act of rebellion expresses nostalgia for innocence and an appeal to the essence of being.

Beauty, no doubt, does not make revolutions. But a day will come when revolutions will have need of beauty.

— *Albert Camus, The Rebel: An Essay on Man in Revolt*

Ernesto "Che" Guevara, or Che, has been the cynosure of youth all over the world because of his intrepid acts that continue to attract the attention of the young and adolescent across the barriers of time and space. It indeed is a painful irony that a devout Marxist who opposed the system of free markets and capitalism has his pictures on clothes and accessories in stores, which are symbols of that very system of oppression against which he fought.

This signifies the tremendous capacity of market forces to absorb seemingly contradictory ideas within their all-encompassing umbrella and render them sterile and impotent.

The legacy of Che is indeed mixed and has drawn responses varying from hatred and derision to unqualified love and adulation. To some, he is a romantic visionary who dreamt of a better world and had the courage to overcome seemingly insurmountable obstacles in his path. To others, he was a bloody murderer who had no qualms in killing or sacrificing any individual at the altar of the revolution. The ends justified the means. Much as there is to admire in him, he leaves behind moral and ethical dilemmas unanswered in his revolutionary zeal. In modern times, to consider him as a role model is to create a demi God with feet of clay.

Back home in India, during the same period that the comet of Che was blazing across the heavens, a couple was applying the principles of Marxism in the tribal belt of Thane district near Mumbai in a more humanistic and peaceful manner, blending the philosophy of Marx and Gandhi in their social laboratory. This couple was Godavari and Shamrao Parulekar who spent many decades in the tribal belt of Dahanu and Palghar organising the Warli tribe against the oppressive mechanism of the landlords, police, courts, and the government in the newly 'politically liberated' India of the late 1940s.

The Parulekars' were both middle class, highly educated people who left the comfortable surroundings they were brought up in to live for decades in conditions that were considered sub-human. Although Shamrao died in the 1960s of a massive heart attack after more than two decades of peaceful nonviolent struggle against the oppressors, his wife Godavari continued the battle against oppression for another three decades until she breathed her last in 1996.

Their struggle may not have blazed across the heavens like that of Che, but the values and principles that formed the basis of this struggle make it more enduring and a better model for the modern age than the bloody warfare waged by Che. The unwillingness of both Shamrao and Godavari Parulekar to sacrifice basic human values and principles at the altar of the revolution was their key contribution to the Marxist praxis and the philosophy of humanism. I read this book in 2003 when I was working with a manufacturing company in Mumbai. I was blown off my feet not only by the simplicity of the prose but by the modest and unassuming manner in which she described the initial days of the struggle and the reluctance of the Warli tribe to fight against centuries of oppression.

The Parulekars' contribution to the political and social paraphernalia and the theory and praxis of Marxism through the organisation of this struggle for more than five decades is immeasurable. But it has unfortunately been restricted to Maharashtra and avid readers of Marxist literature. I thought that the story of this struggle should be made known to non-Marathi audiences and what better way to do that than to translate her immensely popular award winning Marathi book *Jevha Manus Jaga Hoto.* No one but Godavari Parulekar could have written about her own struggle with such passion, insight, deep understanding, humility, and simplicity, I consider myself fortunate to merely have translated her words from Marathi to English so that they reach a wider audience and her struggle receives the recognition and respect it deserves. I am very thankful to Popular Prakashan, Mumbai, for showing the willingness to get this published. If Albert Camus had read about Godavari Parulekar, *The Rebel* might have been different because he would have known a revolution with beauty and justice in it.

— Nikhil Gavankar

I

Background

Forest tribes live in many talukas of Thane district and their numbers are large. They are called *Adivasis* or original inhabitants. The protest against the atrocities by landlords and jungle contractors happened mainly in Umbargaon, Dahanu, Palghar and parts of Javhar talukas. Among *Adivasis*, farmers of the Warli tribe made a major contribution to the struggle. The Warli population is 2,51,851 and makes up about 50 per cent of the total tribal population in this region[1].

A 100 years ago, *Adivasis* were owners of the land and cultivated it. The farms produced enough to satisfy their needs and they enjoyed a good life in the lap of nature. With British rule, and supported by it, came Hindus, Muslims and Parsis from the outside world. They were traders and businessmen and were educated. These outsiders began to cheat the illiterate and naive tribals and grab their lands. Exploiting the *Adivasis'* ignorance, they gradually took control of all the land. They became the owners of the land. These outsiders' methods were corrupt and cruel. Farmers never gladly relinquish their lands. Credible sources say that some farmers were shot dead for their lands while others were tied to trees and whipped or otherwise tortured. Some tribals were conned into putting their thumbprints on papers they could not read and so lost their lands. Morarji Desai, then home minister and revenue minister of Bombay province, described how the *Adivasis'*

1 Keep in mind that this book was written in the 1960s and describes events of the late 1940s and early 1950s. The data is from those periods.

helplessness was exploited to grab their lands. Here are his words from his speech on the law of tenancy farming in the legislative assembly on September 25, 1939:

> *In these tracts like the Bhil tracts in Khandesh district or in the Thana district . . . some years back all the land was held by these people. But in bad times, during the famine or scarcity times, the lands passed from their hands into the hands of the Sowkars for trifling amounts. There are instances in which land has been parted—some acres of land—for 5 lbs. of grain and in some cases at a rate of 5 rupees per acre, or a rupee per acre or 8 annas per acre.*

The then Chief Minister of Bombay province, BG Kher, made similar comments in the Adivasi Seva Mandal (Service Centre) pamphlet dated November 25, 1941.

By 1945 when Warlis started their resistance, only a few owned even small holdings.

The white collar urban class grabbed the land, but they needed the tribals to cultivate it. The tribals reduced to landlessness needed to work for a living. This was the beginning of the slave-like bonded farm labour and inhuman treatment of tribals.

After grabbing all the land, the landlord would give the tribal a small piece of land to cultivate but would keep the most fertile land to himself. In return for the land, the tribal was expected to do all the agricultural work on the landlord's land and that too for free. This is the practice known as *vethbigar* or bonded labour. Simmington, a British government servant, described this free labour as nothing short of slavery. Simmington had been appointed to investigate the conditions of the *Adivasis* and wrote the *Report of the Aboriginal and Hill Tribes, 1939*.

When handing over a small, inferior piece of land to the tribal, the landlord made a contract called *kabulayat* or agreement. Under the contract, the farmer had to give half or even more of the produce from the farm to the landlord. In reality, landlords extracted more than the share stated in the contract. The farmer would get the land only if he agreed to the share the landlord demanded. The tribals were hungry for land, treated it as a piece of their heart and their only source of livelihood. They were willing to do anything for it. The part of produce the farmer handed over to the landlord was called *khand* or *makta*. The farmer who worked under these terms was called *kula*. Landlords engaged in double exploitation. They had their own lands worked free of cost and got a part of the farmer's produce. The farmers did many other odd jobs for the landlord, anxious that they might lose their piece of land if they protested. In the forest areas of Thane district, landlords not only had agricultural lands but also owned grassy lands and held monopoly contracts over forest produce. Farmers worked without wages for landlords, felling trees, cutting grass, and clearing forest tracts.

When I went to work in this region in 1945, *Adivasis* lived in an area of about 1,000 square miles approximately 60 miles from Bombay. This was their world. In Dahanu, Palghar, and Umbargaon talukas, in the jungles and valleys and ravines lived the half naked and ill fed tribals. They knew nothing of the outside world and did not feel the need to find out. In those days, the region had no roads, schools, or hospitals. There was only unimaginable poverty, terrible destitution, suffering, sorrow, disease, and ignorance. Death and exploitation ravaged the region.

Thousands of *Adivasis* lived in such abysmal conditions that it cannot be expressed adequately in words. D Simmington, who reported on *Adivasis*' condition, said in his report, "The conditions under which the jungle tribes people work and live are wretched in the extreme, and [the] abuses to which they are subjected constitute a blot on the administration."

BG Kher, in a paper issued by the Adivasi Seva Mandal on July 1, 1940, says, "The fact that such a big mass of humanity should be rotting in a condition of life more debasing than that of slaves within 50 miles from Bombay and that our citizens should be in complacent ignorance about their hardships and tortures is extremely disgraceful."

People living in cities cannot know the wrecked lives and piteous conditions of the tribals in 1945. In that year, when the exploitation and suffering passed beyond endurance, the tribals rose up to fight even at risk to their lives. The battle lasted two years. With courage and determination they fought the repressive forces of imperialism, indigenous government, and landlordism and won victory in 1947. With this, they earned a place of honour in the Indian farmers' struggle. This never-before struggle attracted the attention of ordinary people, too.

There was much speculation about why and how the struggle happened, about its origins and aims. Some had a clear motive to disparage the struggle and promote misconceptions about it. The national government and national newspapers said that the Warlis being illiterate, uncivilised, and backward, had been led astray by the Communists' inflammatory propaganda, had been induced with lies to take up the fight. I heard many educated, urban people say that the Communists incited Warlis to acts of violence and arson. The Congress government's statement issued on January 13, 1946, contained falsehoods, describing the struggle as "the undesirable activities of those who advocated violence to bring about a political change, namely the ushering of a Communist state in India". To so explain a peoples' struggle is to express contempt for the people and antipathy for those who work among the downtrodden. How else could anyone offer such an analysis of a brave struggle.

The same struggle was described in the foreign newspaper *Australian Daily Telegraph* by reporter Michael Brown in these words: "A woman Communist is leading a revolt of the Aborigines, Warlis, in the thick jungles of Thana District of Bombay." Regardless, it is true that this was the revolt of the *Adivasi* farmers who had been living in slavery for a century.

The proper analysis of the struggle came from a supporter of the Dalit cause and Mahatma Gandhi's follower Narhari Parekh. In *Harijan dated January 19, 1947, he writes:*

> *The riots of the Adivasis (Warlis) in Dahanu Taluka should be an eye-opener to us. No doubt the police and the military will suppress the riots and peace will be restored. But that does not mean that the problem is solved. Such riots are outward symptoms of a serious disease in the body politic. So long as the root cause of this disease is not removed, a superficial treatment of outward symptoms will not be of any avail. These rioters are known to be extremely timid people. Their poverty and ignorance baffle description. For ages they have been exploited by the rulers of the day, by the landlords, the*

> *money-lenders and a host of other parasites. They were the original owners of the land, but today they are forced to labour on the same land as serfs. The new landlords and the moneylenders profit to an unconscionable extent by their labour. At the back of this exploitation, there lurks frightful injustice and suppression. So long as the exploitation, suppression and injustice are not removed, it is futile to hope for a lasting peace . . . . Is it any wonder, if they are exasperated and resort to violence out of a feeling of frustration and despair? The spirit of the exploited and the suppressed people has awakened. The point both in time and circumstance has arrived which demands their full deliverance. None will be able to stop that process.*

This explains why the *Adivasi* had to resort to a desperate struggle. Where did the *Adivasi* find the inspiration to fight with such courage against those who exploited them? What feelings and dreams transformed the meek *Adivasis* into courageous, unflinching warriors? How were they able to withstand torture and make sacrifices? What changed the ignorant, naive, and timid tribals in such a short time? In the pages that follow, I have tried to describe, albeit in my unpolished language, what I saw and experienced, and what I and my co-workers were able to do under Comrade Shamrao Parulekar's guidance and encouragement.

II

Warli Life on the Fringes of Society

The first Maharashtra Kisan Parishad organised by the Maharashtra Kisan Sabha was held in Titwala in Thane district. Comrade Parulekar addressed a public meeting to announce the conference in Dongari village in Umbargaon district. His speeches captivated the Warlis. On his invitation, some Warlis attended the Titwala conference, where a call was given to abolish bonded labour. Encouraged, the Warlis returned to their villages bearing the red flag and resolved to abolish bonded labour. As soon as Warlis declined to do bonded labour, landlords started employing repressive tactics. The question before the Warlis was how to resist these atrocities. They immediately sent for me. Comrade Parulekar, my colleagues, and I decided to call a large public meeting of *Adivasis*. I left for the area immediately to understand the situation.

I did not know much about *Adivasi* life. I had been educated in Pune. My work in the social sphere began in Mumbai. I knew nothing of the tribal region. I was eager to go to Adivasi lands, see a new way of life, and meet new people. Comrade Dalvi and I left for Talasari, where we planned to hold the first meeting. It was a small village and not as well-known then as it is today. Talasari is about 10 kilometres to the east of Sanjan station on Western Railway. When we got off at Sanjan, I saw people racing for the bus as if for life. The bus services were privately operated. If we missed the bus, there would be no bus until the following day. We walked towards the bus wondering how we would find a place. The bus was crowded and people were crushed together. The white collar, well-heeled people sat on the benches while *Adivasis* and the poor were cramped together in the aisle. We added ourselves to them.

We had no idea where Talasari was and where to get off the bus for that village. I thought of how little I knew. We thought we would just get off when the conductor called out "Talasari" or when passengers for that village got off. We would make our way to some farmer's house and then figure out what to do next from there on. I was a little worried since it was a totally unfamiliar area. I had not yet seen how deeply *Adivasis* had been influenced by the Titwala conference, how strongly the downtrodden could be encouraged by even the smallest gesture of support, how much people could sacrifice for their loved ones. I experienced these things later during the many years of struggle.

A little short of Talasari, the road is lined on both sides by huge banyan trees. Groups of *Adivasis* stood under these trees waiting for us. Some carried red flags. Just as I realised it was Talasari, the *Adivasis* stopped the bus and received us.

Meeting at Talasari

Warlis had made handsome preparations for the meeting by their standards. Under a tree was laid a none-too-clean mattress, probably borrowed from some landlord or moneylender, and a piece of rug served as coverlet. A pot of drinking water and a couple of other pots stood nearby. All this was possible only because our enemies did not yet know about us. Such luxuries could never be repeated again during the campaign. Who would lend us a mattress or a rug? On that first day, *Adivasis* gathered around us as soon as we got off and expected us to hold a public meeting immediately.

The Second World War had just ended. A government ruled in the name of a 93-point programme. There was a ban on public meetings. We had not obtained permission to organise the meeting, but the Warlis were eager for it. The dilemma was that if we held the meeting, we would violate the law, and if we did not, we would disappoint the *Adivasis*. I asked casually why they had made such elaborate preparations for a poor people's organisation. Someone explained that they had made the same preparations when BG Kher had addressed a meeting there. I said, "Ours is the poor people's flag and we don't need the mattress and all these things." I then asked to move to a hut nearby. We went to a big hut in Mangalpada in Talasari. We had asked only for the leaders to attend, but everyone followed us in. The hut and compound were packed with people. Some sat on the veranda while others stood in the doorway. The elders sat in the front as is the custom while the others sat at the back. A leaf mat was laid on the floor for us. To begin the meeting, we took out the red flag. But we did not have any pins and wondered how to put it up. Just then, someone got four thorns and pinned the red flag to the wall. This was a pleasing novelty to our city-bred minds. The Warli waited in eager silence to see what would happen. Suddenly, the moneylender's muscleman came brandishing a thick club. The Talathi who was staying with the moneylender as his guest followed the muscleman. The Warlis made way and the two came over straight to us and sat down next to us. The muscleman plonked himself down and put the club on the floor with a thump. The Warlis grew nervous and looked worried. The Talathi and the muscleman sat wearing an expression that said, "We'll deal with whatever happens." They ruled the area in those days. No one had the courage to look them in the eye. The Warlis were nervous because they knew that the muscleman and the Talathi were there to spy on the meeting—to learn what happened, who were present, and what they said. The atmosphere had changed, had become stifled. The landlords' henchmen had to be driven out if Warlis were to speak freely. I told the Talathi that, as he was an employee of the civil authority, he had no right to attend a meeting in a private area without a government order. At this, the Talathi looked at the muscleman. I had to repeat it for the muscleman that they had no right to attend a private meeting in a private place without our permission. I made it more explicit: "I know why you are here. Do not stay here. You go about your business and let us go about ours. Why have you brought this club? Are you scared or do you want to scare others? The days of threatening people with a club are gone." No one had ever spoken to them in such a manner in the presence of Warlis. The henchmen in this backward region were also backward. They were at a loss for an answer. They tried to explain it away: "We just wanted to listen. If you don't want us, we will leave." The muscleman picked up his club and left rolling his eyes. The Talathi followed with his head bowed.

As soon as they left, the mute Warlis broke into speech. Everyone started talking at once and all was confusion. We did not understand it at first. The landlord's muscleman and the Talathi had had to back down and that too in front of Warlis. This had made the Warlis very happy. They saw that there were people who could quote the law to the henchmen and make them leave a meeting. The powerful, too, were afraid of somebody. Warlis had seen this for the first time in their lives. Their joy knew no bounds. The atmosphere of the meeting changed again.

Adivasis who had been waiting to give vent to their sorrows started speaking all at once, some half risen from the floor, others standing up, and yet others sitting. We were surprised at their enthusiasm and happiness. We let them speak their hearts out. Finally, one of them said, "The woman has come to us. Let us listen to her." But I asked them to speak individually and listened with care. They felt strong anger at landlords, moneylenders, their henchmen, the supervisors at work, police officers, forest officials, and officers of the civil administration. They hated these people with a passion that consumed their lives.

With the connivance of these officials, landlords and moneylenders inflicted inhuman repression and brutal treatment on *Adivasis.* The sight of two of these oppressors driven out released the pent up emotions of these poor people. They started describing the injustices they suffered. The presence of sympathetic listeners transformed small incidents into major ones.

When their excitement abated somewhat, doubts crept in. What had happened was good. But what if the muscleman and Talathi came back to harass them again after Madam had left? What could they do? We told them that we would come to their aid if anybody bothered them. This reassured them somewhat. After this, I made a speech in very simple language and explained what the red flag and the Communist Party were.

Adivasis heard the word Communist Party for the first time in this meeting. We had them say this word many times. They learned the word and taught it to others. In those days, they found it difficult to say the slogan, "May the Communist Party be victorious." So we changed it to, "Victory to the Communist

Party." When Acharya Atre visited the area, he met Warlis who said, "I belong to the Communist Party." The red flag was the rescuer of the poor. The flag and the name of the party were imprinted on the Warli heart. They understood and appreciated my argument about the henchmen: The law applies to the henchmen, too, and they have to go when challenged under the law. In this manner, wielding the law like a whip, the red flag would put an end to landlords' oppression and cruelty. I cannot say how much of the rest of the speech they understood. After the speech, everyone started talking at once again. "How they lord it over us. And how they went away like sheep today." We left them saying that we had to go from village to village, unite people, and organise big rallies.

Our work really started only after the speech. After the formal meeting ended, Warlis approached us to tell us of their troubles. They had developed warm feelings for us. When we left, they walked us to the village square, asking for promises of return and saying, "If you don't come back, they will kill us." Many stood in groups talking about what had happened. Those who had been indifferent and had not paid much attention were now talking about the red flag. During the early days of the struggle such incidents—minor to the urban person—won us the confidence of *Adivasis*. At Talasari, we had a glimpse of Adivasi life. The incident demonstrated to *Adivasis* that we were different, our language was different, and we would do something for poor people like them. We left satisfied that we had earned their trust.

We had left Mumbai in the morning on just a cup of tea. We had not planned to stay overnight with the Warlis. Since we were strangers to them, we did not ask Warlis for lunch or tea. This changed later. Warlis gave us meals and tea with affection. On that day, though, we left Talasari for Sanjan station thirsting for a cup of tea. We had to make further preparations for the work ahead. So we resisted the temptation to talk some more with Warlis and left immediately.

When Comrade Parulekar learned about the meeting at Talasari, he immediately decided to hold a large convention at Zari village in Umbargaon district. Comrade Dalvi and I would visit villages in Umbargaon to spread the message.

Tea at Dongari

Comrade Dalvi and I went to many villages in Umbargaon to spread the message of the planned Zari convention. We stayed overnight in some villages, held meetings in others, and addressed rallies in a few. Dongari village is three to four miles to the east of Sanjan station. There were no roads or buses to the village in those days. We ate snacks and drank tea at Sanjan station and then started for Dongari on foot. At around nine in the morning we reached a *pada* in Dongari.

A cluster of 10 to 15 huts is known as a *pada*. A village is made up of five to seven, at most 10, and rarely 15 such *padas* or clusters. The distance between clusters can be anything from half a mile to two to three miles. To visit every such cluster in a village, one had to walk five to six miles. Most clusters were on higher ground and sheltered by trees.

We went to a cluster called Salkar Pada. A bamboo hut was specially prepared for us, with the walls freshly plastered with cow dung. Warlis use little wood in their huts—only for frames, and four or five beams. Some huts don't use even this much. Some huts are so low that one must stoop to enter. One of our Party workers, Laxman Sapata, had such a house, and I had to be very careful going in and out. Most of the houses had only one room and one door. Just cut away a few bamboo sticks in a wall and you had a window. To keep out the rain, grass or leaves made up a roof. Very few houses had tiled roofs.

Since Warlis had no valuables to protect, their huts didn't have to be strong; they would collapse at a kick. A veranda six to nine inches above the ground and edged by stones ran all around the hut. We sat on one of the verandas. In front of every hut was a small bamboo and sticks arrangement like a low table. It bore a pot of drinking water. In the ground around the hut were small holes filled with water for the chicken.

At Dongari, we sat for some time, but there was no sign of life, nobody to be seen. No one came to ask why we were there, what we wanted. All was silent except for bird calls and the chickens' flapping wings. After a while, we got up and walked around. In one place we found a bunch of half-naked, wretched-looking children.

A couple of children who cared for them stood nearby. The boys wore only a loin cloth. The girls were draped up to the thighs in a half or quarter metre of cloth. The children and the barking of dogs were the only signs of human habitation.

I went to some huts. What did I see there? On one side was the rudimentary *chulha*—three stones to keep the pot with the cooking fire in the centre—and a pile of ash in and outside it. An aluminium pot blackened from the fire, a pot or two, a couple of earthenware frying pans or *tavas*, a little rice in a pot, some *ragi* gruel in another, raw turmeric in a pan, a couple of onions, garlic, leaves to roll *bidis*. A foot to foot and a half long piece of bamboo, closed on one end and hung on a wall, held tobacco. This was the jungle equivalent of the jar used to store things.

We went into huts and came out. No one ever objected or asked who we were and what we were doing in the hut. The whole cluster lay lifeless like someone comatose. The decrepit huts, the grinding poverty, and desolation filled me with a sense of unease. I feared that I would lose myself in this lifeless village. Melancholy cast a shadow on my mind. I wondered, what I had got myself into? What would happen? Would I have to accept defeat? Could I cope with the work I had taken up? By now we had walked almost three miles. If we managed to get nothing done, we would have to trudge back that distance again in the heat. I had the tea habit, and knew wouldn't get a cup until we were back at Sanjan station. It drove me nearly to tears. I could recover only because of my faith in my ideology and my passion for the underprivileged. We decided to wait until we met a village elder. We sat on a platform eating some fruits that Comrade Dalvi had gathered from a tree.

Word of our arrival slowly reached the youngsters who were grazing cattle and goats. Children gathered to look at us. Some rested their chins on their sticks and others just stood—and all stared at us. When we asked where the adults were, we learned that they had all—every single one—gone to the landlord to serve as bonded labour. We told a couple of older children, "Go tell the grownups that the red flag people from the Titwala rally are here and have asked you to come here. Bring them back with you." The children exchanged whispers and started on their way. We were left to wonder whether they would deliver our message. The rest of the children left and we were released from their stares. Time passed, but nobody came. In that desolate place, every moment seemed like an hour. Where had the children gone, would they bring anyone back, or would they just wander off—we had no way to know. We spent the time restlessly, getting up and then sitting down again. The forced inactivity was suffocating. I had a bad craving for tea. In the idleness, I felt the hunger and thirst more keenly. Anxiety gripped my mind. Suppressing the storm of emotions in our minds, Comrade Dalvi and I behaved as if nothing was wrong and waited for the Warlis to come.

Warlis tried our patience that day. We were about to go back when we saw the messenger children return with two or three adults following. The sight of the half-naked, long-haired Warlis revived my spirits. They had not been able to come any sooner because the foreman would not let them go. They had stood up to the foreman and insisted on leaving only because they had been told that the red flag people from the Titwala rally had come. Their blank faces expressed no emotions. They greeted us with their traditional form of namaste, which is to rest the right elbow in the left palm and raise the right hand to the nose. They had a brief discussion and then took us to the village school, which was a rectangular hut with mud walls. They did not talk to us. We just stood there. One person swept the floor and another spread a rug for us. I was exhausted and I sat down on the rug, resting my back against the wall. But just then, other Warlis brought a cot. I asked for the cot to be put outside the hut under a tree.

I asked them to gather the village elders. But they could not come in time. All the adults had reported for work as bonded labourers. By the time they got the message and came back, it would be evening. The 10 to 15 Warlis who had gathered sat down along the walls. One of them brought a smouldering piece of wood, another brought *bidi* leaves, and a third gave everyone tobacco from the bamboo jar. Warlis rolled *bidis*, lit them, and sat smoking while wondering what to do with the guests. They knew nothing could be done until people gathered. They did not know what to say to us, how to pass the time until everybody came. Comrade Dalvi and I were talking to each other.

I wanted tea so I asked "Could I have some tea? You know, Dadu, just as you feel a craving for toddy, I feel it for tea. Can something be done?" They had nothing to make tea and could not see a way to solve the problem. One person asked, "Would you like to have lunch?" It was easier for them to make lunch than to make tea. We told them that we would eat whatever they normally had for lunch. They said, "Madam, we are poor people. What can we give you in this jungle?" With these words, they began to work. I thought we would not get any tea, only lunch. But they started making preparations for tea as well as for lunch. Making tea was a big problem for them. They did not have sugar; they did not need it. In any case it was rationed and not easily available. No one had tea powder. There was neither cow nor a buffalo in the village and so no milk. They talked to each other.

First Warli: "Hey, how do you make tea?"

Second Warli: "We can make tea, but what about sugar?"

Third Warli: "We don't have it, but the village headman must have brown sugar."

Second Warli: "His stock is over. But he has jaggery. If he doesn't have it, we will get it from Shivrai."

First Warli: "Madam, would you mind tea with jaggery?"

A child was sent to get jaggery from Shivrai. After some discussion about who had tea powder, another child was sent to buy some tea powder from a shop. I asked how far the shop was and was told that it was close by; the boy would cover it in two strides. Later I learnt that there were no shops within three miles. Their two strides measured a distance of three miles! After the problem of tea and sugar were solved, they remembered the milk. The surprise is that they remembered milk at all. If ever they drank tea, it was always without milk. Drinking milk was unknown. Many did not like milk in their tea, it made them nauseous. They would never even imagine making and drinking tea. Their condition was such that they firmly believed that drinking tea was not for them. I told them that we would take tea without milk, but they could not believe this. They called yet another child and told him 'gather a goat'. The goats from the village were out grazing. The term 'gather a goat' meant find and catch a goat and milk it. The child understood the entire instruction in the words 'gather a goat' and went away to do it. Once arrangements for tea were done, they started making preparations for lunch. Lunch meant another big effort for them.

I saw that the arrangements for tea would take some time, so I lay down on the cot under the tree outside the school hut. Comrade Dalvi stretched out on the leaf mat, called *hataree*, under a tree. We were both tired. We dropped off to sleep almost immediately in the cool breeze under the trees.

The Warlis woke us up with everything ready for tea—jaggery on a leaf, tea powder on another leaf, a pot of clean water, vessel scrubbed clean, and a fire in the three-stone *chulha*. They thought we would not like the tea they made and were pleased when we said we wanted the tea they made. An important person then came forward to make tea. A few others sat around him. The vessel was filled with water and put on the fire. All the tea powder and jaggery they had was added, and then they waited for the milk. In about half an hour, the child came back with the goats' milk in a leaf cone, and the milk was poured in. The gloop was boiled until it turned the colour of tea. They felt that the guests must be served tea first and so it was poured into two small brass cups.

When we asked the Warlis to take tea with us, they rolled leaves into cones and the tea was poured. Thus ten to fifteen persons enjoyed a tea party for just an *anna's* worth of materials.

Comrade Dalvi and I talked among ourselves in English. Taking tea in the company of such educated, white collar people was a new experience to the Warlis, and the pleasure showed on their faces. They gave Comrade Dalvi and me a lot of tea. That tea, or at least something that smelt like tea, made for us with great effort and affection, cheered us up. In those days, the tea in Warli homes was of this kind. Whatever village I visited, I would ask for tea. While the arrangements were made, I would catch some sleep. Many a times, especially in Dubali and Dhodi homes, they used grass extracts instead of tea powder. I could never learn to drink that kind of tea. They later realised that we did not like tea made from grass extracts and would somehow get tea powder. The situation has changed a lot today.

I had my tea and was lying on the cot. Many people were yet to come. I wondered how I had liked the tea when all my life I had drunk tea made by pouring boiling water on Lipton or orange pekoe leaves in a tea pot and then adding fresh milk. The answer is simple. A person who has a goal does not worry about the problems and suffering that must be faced to achieve that goal. In fact, facing problems gives a kind of satisfaction.

The Warlis had been making preparations for lunch. They had never known educated city-bred people to eat lunch with them, sit in their huts, and be one among them. They not only realised that we were different, they saw that we considered ourselves one of them. It helped us win their confidence. It gave them pride where they had only been shunned by society earlier. They wanted to do their best for us. They never had enough to feed themselves but tried to give us a proper lunch. They wore hardly a piece of cloth but were concerned about our sleeping arrangements. They were surprised, and inwardly happy, that we would eat and sleep with them. I thought that we had not yet done anything for those poor people but they already gave us their affection and trust. People who had never been treated like human beings were so hungry for humaneness and support.

It was three in the afternoon by the time arrangements for lunch were complete. By that time most Warlis had assembled in the school. A few who had further to travel were yet to come. The school hut was packed. Sitting crowded together were Warlis in only a loincloth, others in black, embroidered though dirty jackets, some with a handkerchief tied over their heads and others with their hair tied in a topknot. A cooking fire was built and sticks with glowing tips were passed from hand to hand to light *bidis* while others used flint stones.

Landlords in Retreat

Comrade Dalvi raised the red flag and gave a small speech. Then I started to speak. I explained in various ways that Warlis should not perform bonded labour, that the practice has been declared illegal. I described the landlords' atrocities and said that the red flag had come to stop the atrocities. The Warlis did not wait for me to finish my speech but interjected their stories of hellish suffering and helplessness. The stories were unending and a noisy confusion grew. The fact that we would be staying among them encouraged them and the dam of pent up feelings burst. One of them said: "Forget all the other stories. Right now, some of our people are working as bonded labourers for the landlord. The landlord has not allowed them to come here. Please do something about it."

This was a message from the people who had gone to serve as bonded labour. Bonded labourers' carts were kept in readiness on the landlords' estate. Comrade Dalvi went there with a few Warlis. The landlord was there to see to the carts and supervise the farm work. Comrade Dalvi asked him to come outside the house. He declined and asked Comrade Dalvi and the Warlis to go inside. But the Warlis had warned against it and they feared they would be beaten as was the daily practice. So Comrade Dalvi refused to go inside. The landlord would not come out.

The bonded labourers' carts were loaded with firewood, which the Warlis had chopped without any compensation. The cart drivers stood watching. They had to take the wood to the landlord's house five to six miles away in the village of Khattalwad, stack the wood there, and return with the carts. All this work was a part of bonded labour and done free of charge. Comrade Dalvi told the drivers not to move the carts and they complied. When there was no sign of the landlord coming out, Comrade Dalvi sent in the message that the carts would not move unless wages were paid for the trips. The landlord's answer was that no wages would be paid.

Comrade Dalvi told the drivers to unload the wood and take the carts back to their homes. Then he and the Warlis who had gone with him came back to the school. A couple of drivers returned home with the empty carts. The rest remained in the school to see what would happen next. They were uneasy and worried. This was the first time in their lives that they had refused to perform bonded labour for the landlord. It was a new experience to them. They were reassured somewhat by the fact that we would be living with them.

When Comrade Dalvi returned, he was received with excitement and eager questions. He related what had happened. Just then a child relayed the message that the landlord was coming to the school in a *tonga*. Some nervous Warlis got up as if to leave. Even as we talked to them to build their courage and got them to stay, the landlords' tonga raced past the school. The Warlis had feared that their refusal to do bonded labour would, as usual, lead to the landlord abusing and beating them. They had wanted to see whether we would bow down or stand up to the landlord. None of this happened. They saw the landlord slink away. They were exhilarated at this. Young men and children danced and jumped up and down, shouting something unintelligible. To refuse to do the landlord's work and see him meekly accept it was a novel experience to them. As the landlords' tonga went past, the Warlis were stunned into silence for a few minutes at this miracle. They took some time to grasp what had occurred. Some elderly Warlis looked at us. Their eyes twinkled with pleasure and shone with a new awareness.

When their emotional outburst had subsided, I tried to explain our position because this was the right time to put across the message. I used the event to explain, in simple words, that bonded labour was illegal and that they should not perform bonded labour. The atmosphere was not conducive to a long speech. The Warlis were bursting with things they wanted to say. Their joy was bubbling over. One said, "This landlord is usually so overbearing, but today he went away quietly." Another said, "Today he did not hurl abuses at us. He ran away shamed." Everyone was talking, laughing, and making jokes about the landlord. We, too, shared in the happiness.

The incident was actually quite ordinary and unimportant. But it made a deep impact on the Warlis because until then nobody had ever made the landlord back down. This incident proved to be invaluable in gaining the Warlis' confidence. They thought Madam had law in her hands. They did not know that it was the government's law. Even when it was explained, they could not understand it. It was not a part of their life and experiences. They understood the simple truth that the red flag had the power to challenge the landlord and teach him a lesson in law. At that time, it was all they wanted. Discussing the finer points of law was not something they did, were ready to do, or felt they needed to do. They took pleasure in saying again and again how the landlord was made to look a weak fool. By then it was evening and we got up for dinner.

Thick-grained brown rice, red chillies, salt, and raw mango *chatni* was the meal served on leaves. A little *dal* simmered on the fire. As guests we were given seats that were wide logs of wood. The Warlis could not do enough for us. One brought water for us to wash our hands and another scrubbed the wooden seats. One pressed more *chatni* or rice on us while another poured out the boiling dal. We had eaten a little at the station in the morning, but nothing since then. We were very hungry. The atmosphere was full of joy and enthusiasm. We had succeeded in our mission. We ate until we were full. I have never forgotten that meal. It had an extraordinary flavour.

The Warlis too ate with us. Afterwards, we sat on the cot outside the hut. I usually avoided sleeping in the Warlis' huts; the smell of cattle kept me awake. Outside, people gathered again. They had many questions. We had a frank, open talk. These informal sessions were more useful than formal meetings. During the conversation, I reiterated that Warlis should not do any work for free for anybody. If anybody raised a hand, no matter who it was or how big, they should grab that hand before it could strike. The law gives everyone the right to act in self-defence and resist violence. The aggressor should be taken to the police station and we should be informed. There was nothing illegal in this. I also told them that everyone should attend the rally at Zari to make a strong display of unity. They had misgivings about what would happen to them when Madam went away. What would they do if the moneylender threatened them or tried to beat them? They liked the idea of stopping the hand raised against them. But they had lived so helpless and repressed that they did not believe they could do it. We told them that we would be in nearby villages for a few more days and that made them feel a little better. They said, "Madam, if you help, we will find the courage to act. We will demolish bonded labour."

The Warlis went on talking among themselves long after we went to sleep. The next morning, two of them escorted us to our next stop. The others stood watching until we disappeared from sight.

After this stay at Dongari, Comrade Parulekar and I often explored the area on our own without a guide. Word had spread of the incident at Dongari and that we were in the area. Any Warli we met on our walks would have a good idea of who we were, which was confirmed when we introduced ourselves. They would willingly act as guides. We generally travelled early in the morning or in the evening. With an early start, we could visit a village, gather people, hold a meeting, and make it to the next village in the evening. But if we were late getting to a village, people would have already left for work.

Bath at Kajali Village

In those desolate villages, it was very difficult to wait for people to gather with nothing to do. In cities, there are so many things one can do while waiting for someone at a home—newspapers, magazines, books, decorative pieces in the showcase, or the people around. But in the *Adivasi* huts, you would not see so much as a piece of paper or a pencil, leave alone other means of entertainment. Nor did I want to go out in the hot afternoon sun. So I was forced to sit outside the hut for hours, brooding on the miserable lives. Time stood still; I grew desperate, felt distressed.

All this could be avoided if we reached a village in the morning or in the evening. Nature laid out its beautiful treasures as if to welcome us. One might ask why we could not take newspapers or books with us? But we hardly had the energy to read after walking seven to eight miles along a dusty road on just a cup of tea.

A newspaper lasted one day. A book would add to the luggage we had to carry. We were not used to walking seven to eight miles. When it grew hot, we would be miserable by the time we reached the next village. We carried our own luggage, Comrade Dalvi's cloth bag and my small suitcase. We never made Warlis carry our luggage. If we had done that, they would have thought that we, too, used them as bonded labourers.

We took only as much necessary luggage as we could easily carry over seven to eight miles. If the sun grew too strong, I rested the bag on my head for shade. Under the circumstances, I was reluctant to carry books or any extra luggage. I packed only necessary items.

We started a bit late for Kajali village. We could feel the sun beginning to scorch. To make it worse, we lost our way and had to walk longer. On the way, we saw a large bungalow. On inquiring, we learnt that it belonged to a moneylender. We approached and heard the sounds of domestic work. The landlord was not staying there. We went in and sat there for a while. The Warlis working there gave us a drink of water and later some tea without milk. They had guessed who we were, but did not let on. Out of fear, they did not talk either. We were refreshed by the tea and walked faster. Soon we reached Kajali village.

I often could not make arrangements to take a bath. Sometimes I went two or even three days without being able to have a bath or comb my hair. When I felt very dirty, I washed my hands and feet with a little water. Then I felt a bit better. After two to three days of walking about villages, the body would be so grimy and dusty that no city-bred person would have wanted to even stand next to me. Even a bath made little difference. After walking for two or three miles, I would be bathed in sweat. The wind blew the dust which stuck to the skin and matted the hair. Since we had lost our way and reached Kajali late, we decided to bathe first. I still remember the bath I had there.

I reached the village at about eleven in the morning drenched with sweat. If I rubbed the skin, the dirt came off in visible lumps. My clothes reeked of sweat. My *pallu* was so dusty that it didn't absorb the sweat when I tried to wipe with it. My body was steaming in the heat. My feet ached from all that walking. I was at the end of my tether. I managed to hold out until a woman came out of a hut. As soon as she came, I asked for some water to wash myself. She said there was water at a place nearby and we would go there. She thought we would have a lot of water if we went to the source. The Warli woman walked ahead and I followed her with fresh clothes, soap, and towel. We talked as we walked about 500 metres to the so-called water source. What did I see there! A stagnant pool of water covered with green moss! I had walked in hopes of plentiful water, and the green layer brought tears to my eyes.

I asked if that was the water for the bath. She nodded and began to push aside the green layer of moss with a stick. To her, the water below the moss was clean and she began to fill a pot with it. It made me shiver with distaste. I could not face the idea of bathing in that water. I was used to a spacious bathroom with plenty of hot water. The woman understood my reluctance. There was a hole dug below the level of the pool. The water seeped into this hole, getting filtered as it did. She suggested that I used that water. It took some time for the pot to fill. We talked while she collected the water in the pot. There was no mug or anything else to pour the water. I folded myself and crouched on a stone. Using a little water, I soaped myself. Then I crouched and the woman dripped the water on me.

I had had a bath after two or three days and that with just a pot of water, but I managed to clean myself thoroughly. I put on fresh clothes and felt better. Before we turned back, the Warli woman pushed aside the green moss and filled the pot from the pool. Again a shiver passed over me. What could be done? There was no other source of water in the village. For years, people had used that water for washing. Only drinking water was taken from a stream below the village.

The Warli Diet

By the time I returned from my bath, it was afternoon. Some Warlis had come back home. I knew it would take time for lunch. Making lunch began with threshing the paddy to get the rice. If they had no paddy, they had to bring it from somewhere. All this took time. When I entered the hut, I saw children eating gruel out of earthen bowls. On asking, I learnt that it was their afternoon meal. My idea of lunch was rice, dal, a slice of lemon, ghee, two vegetables, chapatis, a sweet, something fried on the right, curds—all eaten with relish—and curd-rice at the end without which a meal was incomplete. With such an idea of lunch, I could not understand how the gruel could be called lunch. I was shocked at what the children were eating.

The gruel was usually made of finger millet (*ragi*) or samo (*wari*). The flour was soaked in water and kept in a pot overnight. The dough fermented the next morning. More water was added and it was cooked and left in the pot. In the afternoon, when the woman returned home from work, she ladled out the gruel to the children and men. The ladle was made of half a coconut shell attached to a stick. The gruel was their afternoon meal. I have seen children lick their plates clean of the gruel. I had also seen children who were fed milk and tonics. The thought raised a storm of emotion in me. I wanted to close my eyes and shut away the misery. The abject poverty disgusted me.

I took some gruel in a leaf bowl and asked the children, "Is this enough?" They replied, "What is the use of saying it is not enough? Sometimes we don't even get this. Then we have to live on roots and leaves."

"What! Do you eat leaves?"

'Yes Madam, leaves of tamarind and red sorrel called *ambadi*. Raw mangoes if we can get them in the season, the *karvanda* berries, *moha* flowers, *arbi* roots, bitter onions, and whatever else we can find to fill the belly."

During the lean season, their only food was bitter onions. These grow in the jungle and the Warlis are constantly in search of the vines. They call it searching for a grain. They find and dig out the root of the vine. Some of the roots are big, but the taste is always bitter. The Warlis slice the roots into thin wedges, wrap them in cloth, and leave them under a stone at the edge of a stream or river. The bitterness is washed out to some degree. The slices are then cleaned with ash and washed and boiled in water. The bitter water is thrown away and the slices are cooked to eat. Most Warli homes have these bitter roots.

Arbi grows in plenty during the rains in the Warli villages. The sight of the big leaves makes a city-bred person's mouth water at the thought of the fried, stuffed rolls made of them. Some urbanites who went with me to this area would say, "What lovely *arbi* leaves. Can we take some? We will pay, of course." Warlis were amused at this but did not like the talk of money. Even in crushing poverty, they were not greedy for a few *annas*. They would not take even a few *annas* from their guests. By comparison, the middle class people offering to pay seemed objects of pity to me.

Warlis did not eat the leaves or stems of *arbi*. They did not know how to use it. They did not have the ingredients to make the vegetable or fried rolls. They did not have so much as a drop of edible oil. When they made dal for us, they used salt, turmeric, and chillies. They did not know *tadka* or seasoning in oil. What use were *arbi* leaves to them in the absence of the other ingredients? They threw away the leaves and cooked and ate the root. They planted *arbi* only for the root. They happily gave away the leaves to anybody asking for them. The arrogant urbanites would say, "Such ignorant people. They don't appreciate the value of the leaves." Little did they know the inside story. You had to be born an *Adivasi* to understand.

That afternoon in Kajali, we spoke about the Warlis' undernourished condition and their diet of roots and about the rally planned at Zari. Then we got up for lunch. They had prepared a special meal for us. There was a hot *bhakari* made of lima bean (*patani*). I wished I had some ghee or butter with the *bhakari*, but that was impossible. We ate red chilli chutney with the *bhakari* and then we were on our way to the next village.

Husk Bhakari at Savai Village

We had not intended to stay at Savai. But it was evening by the time we reached there, and we were tired from walking for miles. The Warlis advised that one should not travel further on foot so late in the evening. We stayed with a Warli who was known to our escorts. We were unexpected guests. The owner was not at home. As was our habit, we sat outside the hut on a rug. Two Warlis started making preparations for dinner. Another Warli went away to announce that we were at Savai.

The hut where we were to stay was so small that one had to bend to enter it. I talked to the Warli for a few minutes and then went into the narrow front room of the hut to see who was at home and what was going on. In a clean vessel, rice was being cooked for us. The man of the house sat leaning against the wall smoking a *bidi.* I went into the inner room and the sight that greeted me stabbed at my heart. The woman of the house sat there with her half-naked children with the round bellies of malnutrition. Near her was a pot in which she had boiled a little rice, a couple of roughly chopped onions, a little salt, and a pot of water. The woman was serving the thin soup to her children. As they emptied their plates, she would ladle out some more. The children slurped the water and ate with relish the few grains of rice and pieces of onion. When Warlis have dried fish, they add it to this soup. When the children had eaten their fill, they lay down tired on the floor. But the woman remained sitting because I was there. I asked, "Have the children eaten enough? They seem to be asleep."

The woman said, "They have to sleep on an empty stomach. What can we do?"

"Today's meal is taken care of. What will you do tomorrow? There doesn't seem to be any *ragi* gruel."

"There is some grain husk and a *bhakari* left over from the morning. I will make some more tomorrow morning."

I took a piece of the husk *bhakari* and went outside. In my travels in those days, I often saw children eating husk *bhakari* and salt for lunch.

The sight brought tears to my eyes. I remembered my childhood when we children used to devour boxes of chocolates and biscuits. A storm of thoughts raged through my mind. How different was that world! It was our country and our people, but what a difference! I went outside to hide my tears.

Much later, Comrade Dalvi and I sat down to eat. The man of the house did not join us. He would eat later with the Warlis who had come with us. We knew by then that Warlis let us eat as much as we wanted and then made do with whatever food was left, though pretending to have eaten their fill. We rarely saw people who ate enough even of their diet of rice, *bhakari*, rice soup, or *ragi* gruel. They ate without complaint their share, which depended on how much food there was and how many were to eat. Not complaining had become second nature. They did not imagine that they had a right to a full meal. We noticed this during the early days of the struggle when five to seven people ate their meals together. They would always insist that we have our meals before them. We did not want to hurt their feelings, so we never insisted that they eat with us.

I had taken some husk *bhakari* to find out what it tasted like. But I hesitated to eat the *bhakari*, which had been kept in the open in a hut with sticks-and-mud walls. How could I put it in my mouth no matter how much I tried? I roasted the *bhakari* on the fire under the pretext of heating it for the meal and consoled myself that the fire had killed any germs it had. I began to eat it. There was some whole rice husk that was hard to chew. I wondered if it would score my intestines. But then I thought that if even small children eat it and come to no harm, why would it hurt me? I determined to eat the *bhakari* no matter what and did eat it. We quickly finished our meals. It was difficult to force down the rice and dal when we could see the ill-fed people, especially the children. But if we had not eaten, the Warlis would have felt bad.

They had brought brinjals, dal, and rice especially for us from somebody living near Sanjan station. They would have thought that the guests did not like the lunch that they had made with so much trouble. If we had not eaten, they would have felt bad at the waste of food. We told them, "We don't do physically strenuous work. So we eat less. We feel full." So saying, we ate a little dal and rice and finished our meal.

When they heard that I had taken husk *bhakari*, some *Adivasis* came to see me eating it. Somebody would turn his head away from the sight and walk away in a rush. One of them said, "Why are you eating husk *bhakari* just to please us? Why do you punish yourself?" But they also thought that these people really care about us that they do not hesitate to eat our food, even a husk *bhakari*. This feeling showed in their behaviour again and again. Some old people sighed on seeing me eat the husk *bhakari* and lowered their eyes. Some had tears in their eyes. This emotion in people who had to eat husk *bhakari* day after day wrung my heart. I did not know what to say.

We sat outside the hut and talked for a long time, and then one by one everybody fell asleep there in the open. I lay down but could not sleep. I kept seeing the children wolfing down thin rice soup while their parents, the farmers, toiled day and night to bring riches of food out of the earth. I began to wonder whether our efforts could change this state of affairs. Or would things go on as they were? Would I live to see a change? Today, I can see it as if it happened only yesterday. But today I can take some satisfaction in the fact that things have changed. The most important thing is that the king of the jungle, the *Adivasi*, has awakened.

Ambadi or Roselle Leaves Vegetable

One day I was walking alone in the jungles near the mountains to the east of Dahanu. A young cowherd showed me the way up the mountain behind a clump of trees. I took a walking stick and began the climb and made it to the top by the evening. At the top, I met a boy about 13-years-old. His village and home were nearby. I went with him to his house to spend the night there. By the time we had climbed down the mountain and reached his house, it was dark. Cooking fires burned in every home. The boy's name was Vithu Karabat. He took me home with great warmth and affection. His father had gone out, but his mother was at home. Vithu went out to get a cot for me. Another child went to bring his father. Vithu soon returned with the cot, and I laid a leaf mat on it and sat down. Vithu's father came back. Everybody was worried about dinner. It was already dark. What preparations could they make for dinner? The parents and the child held a whispered discussion. I told them quite firmly, "I will eat whatever you have cooked for yourselves. I don't eat some special kind of food." That solved the delicate problem, and the woman went inside the house.

I talked to Vithu. He was educated to the fifth standard. In those days, one rarely met children who could even read and write. Vithu and his father started talking to me, "Your coming to our home today is like God coming here. God sent you here." I did not understand what he meant by this. I thought it was the usual form praise for the guest: "You are godly people and we are blessed that your feet touched our house." But it was not that. The Talathi was harassing the family, and they believed that I would be able to set things right. Vithu's father had paid his dues to the landlord. But the landlord said that, according to his accounts, the Warli—Vithu's father—still owed him money. The Warli insisted pleadingly that he had paid the share and the payable in the landlord's accounts was a lie. The day I went to Vithu's place happened to be the day when the Talathi had taken away what little paddy was in Vishu's house as payment of the landlord's share. Even after that, the landlord was claiming more was owed. If the remainder was not paid, he had threatened to take away everything in the house—pots and pans, the beams of the hut, the plough and all the rest. Vithu's family was frightened and worried. When I had reached the home, Vithu's father had gone to discuss the problem with the elders in the village. By the law, pots, pans, plough cannot be seized for recovering dues. But the landlord and the government officials obeyed no laws and ruled by brute force. The landlord's word was the law; he was the ruler.

The Warlis took succour in the fact that I had gone there at the time of this difficulty. Vithu could read and write and his accounts and calculations were accurate. But that was no use in the face of the combined forces of civil authorities, police, and the landlords. Even when a poor man is educated, that education has no value in the brutal regime of the landlords.

On making enquiries and checking the details of the case, I concluded that the Adivasi was right. I wrote a strongly worded letter to the Talathi. I told the villagers that if the Talathi tried to use force, a dozen or so of them should come forward and tell him, "Your actions are illegal, and we will not allow you to lay a finger on the hut." If that was not enough to stop him, I told them to send me a message, wherever I was in that area. Soon many more people gathered and I explained what to do to them. Challenging the Talathi was new to them and they did not have the confidence to do it. They were worried and discussed it among themselves.

Dinner was ready and we went back to the hut. The hut was so small that one had to enter it almost sitting down. The hut was very small and the cooking fire burned strongly. As it was too hot inside the hut, we decided to eat outside. On a plate was served rice and sour leafy vegetable (*ambadi*). The vegetable was so hot and sour that I was loath to put it in my mouth. It was just ambadi leaves boiled in water with salt and red chillies. But I had no choice but to eat.

The Warli had asked with tears in his eyes whether I could eat that food. They felt deep regret that poverty prevented them from serving me anything better. The plate of rice was brought out emitting a sour smell. I gave back most of the rice. The sour water from the vegetable had soaked the rice. I managed to push a little rice and vegetable down my throat and finished the meal. But the sour flavour remained in my mouth. The Warlis were happy that I had eaten with them.

While I was eating, they had discussed the matter and had decided to send my letter to the Talathi. We chatted of this and that and then I lay down on the cot. The Warlis slept in the open courtyard.

In those days, hardly a home had light. There were no lanterns, but a rare home had a small oil lamp. Failing that, a wick run into a bottle served as a lamp. Most Warlis went about their daily routine by the light of a campfire outside the hut or the cooking fire inside it. During the winter, they slept near the campfire for warmth. If they needed light inside a hut, they took a burning piece of wood and used the light for whatever they needed to see. There was no dearth of firewood; they brought it from the jungle.

I was awakened in the night and saw Vithu's mother sleeping behind my cot. I saw that her *sari* did not have a *pallu* that goes across the chest and over the shoulder. I had noticed that many Warli women's *saris* did not have the *pallu*. I had asked around and some women said their *saris* were four yards long and others said their *saris* were five yards long. I had the fixed notion that a Marathi *sari* was nine yards long. I asked a shopkeeper about this once when I was in the market at Khattalwad village. He said, "Warlis cannot afford to buy a nine yard *sari*. We get *sari*-like cloth with borders, and cut out as much length as they ask for. They buy as much as they can afford to." I remembered this explanation when I saw Vithu's mother that night.

The sound of the train at Dahanu woke me up. On one side were the mountains covered with dense forest. From a distance came the sounds of the train. Warlis lay asleep on the ground around the courtyard. Those bare bodies lying any which way brought home the horror of their condition. How could man reduce man to such abysmal conditions? All around was silence and stillness. I couldn't sleep. What would be the outcome of what had happened? What trials did we still have to face? Would the condition of these poor, blameless people ever improve? These and other such questions made me restless. At the same time, I took pleasure in the way my life was being enriched by new experiences.

I fell asleep towards dawn, when a cool breeze began to blow, thinking of how I would narrate the story of my travels and what Comrade Parulekar would think of it.

I washed my face in the morning and was ready to go to the next village. Warlis walked with me quite a long distance, saying, "If there's trouble, you have to come back." They said it again and again with me saying yes. Two days later, I heard that, on reading my letter, the Talathi had talked abusively, stomped his feet, and gone away fuming. Nothing else happened. The news of this incident spread like wildfire in the area. The Warlis' confidence in us grew.

I had a glimpse of the life of Warlis who lived on *ragi* and other grain gruel, thin rice soup, husk *bhakari*, tamarind and *ambadi* leaves, bitter onions; had hardly enough clothes to cover themselves; owned a few pots and pans; and lived in the sad, desolate huts in the jungles. I was introduced to the poor, helpless farmers. Their suffering and misery wrenched at my heart, made me melancholy. Before going to the Warli area, I had read that the Indian farmer was poor and culturally backward. I had also learned from Comrade Parulekar who had made a deep study of the conditions of the farmers. I had some idea of the state of affairs. But when I actually went there and saw the impoverishment, I was stunned. I felt ashamed of myself when I saw their poverty and backwardness. These are citizens of the same country, our brothers and sisters! They live a mere three hours by rail from Mumbai! Why had I never heard the sad story of these people being denied even their human status? I had to hang my head in shame. My husband, Comrade Parulekar, and I pledged that we would work tirelessly to break the chains of bondage of these farmers, bring them out of their hellish existence and awaken the human being inside them. We have been able to fulfil the pledge thanks to the efforts and unflinching loyalty of thousands of Warlis and others.

III

Affluence of the Landed Class

On one side were Warli farmers who wanted food, clothing, medicines, and education, and had no recourse to justice when they were beaten or even killed. On the other side were the rich landowners who lived in arrogant luxury.

During the early years, I did not have an opportunity to visit the mansions of the rich and observe their lives. We were unwanted from the beginning because the landowners had preconceived notions against Communists. During our struggle in 1945-47, I gained some understanding of their lives.

The landlords typically had two residences. One was to the west of, and near Western Railway stations such as Sanjan, Khattalwad, Umbargaon, Bhilad, Shirgaon, Gholwad, Dahanu, Vangaon, Palghar, Boisar, Chinchani, and Tarapur. They have their big bungalows in these villages and live there. On the eastern side are their farmlands. For short stays to supervise farm work, they have farmhouses, which might be anything from a small hut to a large bungalow. The landlords' exploitative reach radiated from these farmhouses out into the forest and into Warli huts. The landowners' farmhouses were symbols of the oppression and brutal treatment of the impoverished *Adivasis*.

In October 1945, I had occasion to enter a landlord's home for the first time. *Adivasis* had gone on strike and they had been fired on. To discuss the question of labourers' wages, the district collector Bedekar had invited Comrade Parulekar and me to Homi Daviyarwala's palatial bungalow at Sanjan.

Palatial Bungalow

The bungalow was set back about 50 metres from the gate and the path to it was laid with fine sand. It was a spacious two-storied building surrounded by gardens with flowering plants and other trees. On climbing the steps, the visitor came to a wide veranda and then a large hall inside. The staircase to the upper floors was clean and covered with a cloth. The upper floor had a dining table equipped with western gadgets and conveniences and a sideboard laden with fruits and drinks. Though I could not see the entire bungalow, I got a fairly good idea of what the rest of it must be like.

The landlord was a barrister from London and an honorary magistrate in the Umbargaon court. His foreign travels had not made the slightest dent in his feudal and traditional outlook. Only his exterior—his lordly behaviour—had changed somewhat. He had another bungalow on his farm at Vakas. Vakas was a small, backward village. I don't remember if it even had a shop.

From the Sanjan-Talasari road near Kavad village, a road branches off and goes to Vakas. This is the road constructed especially to go to the 'Seth's house'. This bungalow was on raised ground and had a spacious hall with rooms on either side and a veranda front and back. A little way at the back was a kitchen and a storage room. The bungalow had plentiful water supply and all the luxuries and conveniences of a modern lifestyle. There were kerosene and decorative lamps. Around the bungalow were flowering plants and fruit trees.

To one side of the bungalow was a chawl about 35 feet wide and maybe 200 to 250 feet long. There was a broad veranda in front of the chawl. Though there were rooms in the chawl, it was not for poor people to live in. It was the Seth's godown. Different kinds and qualities of grains were stored in different rooms. I cannot quite estimate it even today, but it must have amounted to thousands of tonnes of rice. Nearby were the stables of *pucca* construction and tiled roofs for the landlords' cattle numbering in the hundreds.

The bungalow was on raised ground and gave a view of the land stretching at the back, thousands of acres of farm land, orchards of fruit trees, and flower gardens. From this height of prosperity, one could also see the fires in the huts of hundreds of impoverished Warlis. The Warlis in those huts were the Seth's tenant farmers and bonded labourers. I used to marvel at how the affluence as if of Kuber, treasurer to the Gods, and mind-numbing poverty lived side by side. City visitors to the bungalow enjoyed the landlords' prosperity and hospitality, the beauty of the countryside, and returned praising the landlords' generosity and kindness. They made the pleased comment, "This place has the fun of a village with the convenience of a city." The bonded labourers heard this as they toiled at their work and burned in anger and envy.

Landlords had built bungalows in places far from not only railway stations but even bus stops. Ashta and Raipur were such villages where landlords stayed to maintain their hold over *Adivasis.*

Kochai village is on the border of Nagarhaveli, and holds the symbols of landlord's prosperity. The landlord Maneckji Kochaiwala has a big bungalow there. On the way from the bungalow to the village, there is a stream. The landlord has built a bridge across the stream and it cannot be used without his permission. During the struggle for the liberation of Nagarhaveli, it had rained incessantly and the stream was swollen. Warlis smuggled me over the bridge and were abused for it though they escaped being beaten.

Since Maneckji had never been abroad, his idea of luxury was that of a typical feudal lord. The house had plentiful grain stores, fruits, hens and eggs, and milk. Women in traditional Parsi clothes chatted about *papad*, pickles, and *poha.* Branching from the Talasari-Vapi road, a road was specially constructed to go right to this bungalow. The vast land stretching on both the sides of the road gave an idea of Maneckji's wealth. His supervisor was a Pathan. He treated the *Adivasis* with extreme cruelty and brutality. He was killed during the resistance.

In Kochai, Vankas, and other villages, landlords were unofficial kings enjoying a life of luxury. Villages near the station had the big houses of Hindu as well as Muslim moneylenders. The houses had their horses, carriages, grain stores, and their families. They had food and milk in plenty. While they feasted on rich food, the bonded labourer Warlis worked around them like automata.

The outlook of Hindu and Muslim landlords was feudal and they loved gold ornaments, silverware, and stocks of grain. They did not have even the merely outward modernity of Parsi and Irani landlords. They were orthodox with not a touch of progressiveness. They lived narrow, self-centred lives.

Most landlords had mistresses and used *Adivasi* women as if they were property. Their ideas of morality were orthodox and decadent.

I will never forget one time when I stayed in a landlord's house. Comrade Dalvi and I were standing near Sanjan station watching the crowds at a ration shop. We did not have anywhere to stay that night. We planned to pass the night in the railway station waiting room and go on to the next village the following morning. One of the rich landlords came to where we were standing. He had known my late father Laxman Raghunath Gokhale and recognised me. He invited us to spend the night at his home with the idea of making me see sense and persuading me to stop my work.

We had nowhere to go and accepted. After tea and the usual pleasantries, he started telling us about the backwardness of *Adivasis* and how they needed schools and hospitals—in other words, constructive work. We heard him out. At about 8 o'clock, he got up and said with a laugh that he was leaving to pray to Mahatma Gandhi. I was surprised. Later I learned that he meant he was going for drinks. I never had stayed with a person who drank; it was a novelty to me. I was a little frightened. Comrade Dalvi and I stayed up that night talking. I began to regret going to such a man's home.

We sat down to tea the next morning. There was *poha* and sweet *sheera* with tea, which an *Adivasi* woman brought on a tray. Her children were playing near the landlord. I asked who had made the *sheera*. The landlord pointed to the woman and laughingly said, "Her, my woman," using the rural word for wife. The woman quickly went inside at this remark.

A wave of disgust and anger swept over me at the thought of the Seth's relations with the woman, his readiness to talk about it, and the kind of life it was.

Adivasis' Distress

Even in small villages, landlords had huge, well-furnished houses while *Adivasis* lived in decrepit huts. On one side was the glow of kerosene and petroleum lamps and on the other was the flicker of the fires lit for light and warmth. On one side were feasts with fish from the ponds built with unpaid *Adivasi* labour, eggs from the hens reared by *Adivasis*, and sweets made of milk *Adivasis* carried over 10 miles and more. On the other side were *Adivasis* living on bitter roots, *moha* flowers, leaves, *ragi* gruel, and husk *bhakari.* Landlords would be enraged at any delay in their breakfast of tea, bread, eggs, and sheera or *poha. Adivasi* men and women got up in the morning, had nothing to eat, and left for work.

My own stomach churned at the thought of *Adivasis* who worked from morning to noon without taking a morsel of food. On one side were men in clean *pyjamas, dhoti,* shirts, singlets, or suits and women in silk or superior cotton *saris.* On the other side were *Adivasi* men in loincloths and women barely able to cover their bodies. Landlords sat chewing betel nut and sipping tea and gossiping, while Warlis daily carried loads over distances of 10-15 miles. On one side were godowns filled with food grains and on the other side were *Adivasis* making do with a few grains of rice in a pot of water. Never had I seen such a naked display of opulence alongside grim poverty.

These experiences gave me a hatred for the landlords and a hostility born of that hatred. I badly wanted to teach them a lesson. But I was also angry at Warlis who suffered in silence as if dead in spirit. But when I reflected quietly, I realised that inside them was a volcano ready to explode. Their apparent calm was like ashes on embers. It was my job to blow away the ashes and let the embers burst into flames.

IV

Crimes against Warlis and the Repressive Machinery

When stories of *Adivasi* rebellion started appearing in newspapers so did stories of the atrocities they suffered. But the common person in urban areas remained unaware of the *Adivasi* life. An educated city bred person would comment, "Oh, those Warlis or some such name. You work among them, don't you? I have heard your name. They have been suffering quite badly, it seems." Another would say, "Don't they live in the jungle? They have a lot of problems, don't they? [As if the problems were because of the jungle.] Did you actually go into the jungle?" These remarks showed that ordinary people did not know about the heart-wrenching crimes committed against *Adivasis*. What were the inhuman crimes that would chill a civilised person's heart?

Whenever I stayed in an *Adivasi* home, there was one typical scene. I would be sitting on a cot, the Warlis would be smoking *bidis*, and we would talk late into the night. They would tell me about what had been happening and ask questions. Through these discussions, I learnt a great deal about many aspects of the lives of farmers and the landlords.

Once I visited Bordi village in Umbargaon taluka. The people had invited me to their village. I always accepted such requests. People felt better when I went to their village and they told me their troubles. In many cases, my visit would help stop a landlord's illegal exploitative practices and encouraged *Adivasis*. So I had many invitations from villages. Warlis were happy to receive me although they never showed it. They were not demonstrative. It was not easy to fathom what was on their minds. When I approached a village, *Adivasis* bent over their work would look up at me. When they learnt that I was staying, their eyes would express their pleasure. They would discuss amongst themselves whom I would stay with, and the host-to-be would hand over the work tools to someone and leave for home. But they still did not talk much.

Tightening Screw of Bonded Labour

The landlord had a house in Bordi and he demanded that every day some tenant farmers work for him as bonded labourers. To make sure of attendance at work, an iron rod was used, which the farmers called 'axel of the bond'. Whoever received the rod and all his family members had to work for the landlord for the entire day. When they returned home at night, they would pass the rod to another farmer. The next day, all the members of that family had to report for work. This went on throughout the year. It had been the practice for generations. *Adivasis* knew the rod would come to their home one day and they would have to work for the landlord the entire day for no wages.

The person in whose home I was to stay in Bordi had received the rod. Members of the household had no choice but to go to work. I reached the hut late in the evening and finding no women, asked the husband, "Where is the woman of the house? Where is your wife?" The man and his son exchanged a glance. I guessed that something was wrong but did not know the problem. I went into the hut and saw a woman lying in a corner burning with high fever.

On seeing me, she tried to get up. I told her not to get up and rest because she was ill. I was about to go out when she started weeping. Having received the rod, the entire family had to report for work. Because the woman was ill, she did not go. This enraged the landlord and he sent his supervisor to the hut. The supervisor stormed into the hut shouting abuses and punched her on the back and dragged her out of the hut. The woman grappled with him, but ineffectively. He went back in and to the loft, where he scattered the little paddy the family had stored. The woman wept and begged to be spared. But she was dragged to the landlord's house and told, "You are faking the illness. You don't want to work, just want to get everything for free." She was made to work but fainted with the fever. The landlord asked the husband to take her back home. He took her to the hut but went back to work immediately or he would have been beaten. This was the situation when I reached there, and the woman burst into tears on seeing me. The villagers were angry and had talked about it, but only in whispers. They could not see a way out. So, though they understood what was going on and burned in anger, they went on working without protest.

I stayed the night in Bordi and left for the next village the following morning. That night, I talked to the villagers: "No one should work as bonded labour again. The woman who is ill absolutely must not be sent to work. Quote me if the landlord disagrees. If they use force, send word to me."

In Vasa village, I was to stay with a farmer called Rupaji. He knew I was coming and had rustled up tea, milk, and sugar. I protested, "Rupaji, why make all these arrangements for me. You know I drink tea without milk and with jaggery." He quickly said, "All these days, we lived in fear of the landlord, taking beatings and going hungry. Now that the red flag has come here, we get at least thin rice soup. Can't we even make tea for you? Today, I can eat the mangoes off the trees I planted on my own land. But there was a time when I was beaten to a pulp for eating a single mango."

He then told me the story. When the mangoes began to appear on the trees, the landlord sent a watchman. To prevent anyone knocking off the fruit by throwing stones, they spread thorns around the tree. Rupaji could not resist the temptation to eat a raw mango. Thinking there was no one around, he plucked a ripening mango and started eating it. The watchman appeared out of nowhere and punched Rupaji on the back. He gripped Rupaji by the arm and marched him to the landlord. The mango was presented as evidence of the crime. The Seth asked Rupaji to make a rope from fibrous plant stems. The landlord and the watchman took him to the mango tree and tied him to it with that same rope. He was whipped until his back was lacerated and bled. He screamed like an animal from the pain, but no one could find the courage to go to his aid. The landlord was cold-hearted and the cries had no effect on him.

In those days, most landlords kept whips in their houses. At the slightest protest from Warlis, they used the whips. The whips hanging in the veranda were a constant reminder to Warlis of their slavery. Warlis described it as "The landlord pounds." The expression was exact; landlords' beating was like pounding and clobbering. Landlords had got used to beating and locking up Warlis with or without reason. Whipping and abusing Warlis was routine the way cleaning the house is routine. Landlords had not the slightest feeling that beating a fellow human being was barbaric and abased the person doing the beating. "The pigs have to be thrashed," they said, treating the beatings as a part of their power as landlords. Their ingenuity had gone into devising cruel methods of torture other than beatings.

Once a landlord wanted to redraw the borders of a tenant farmer's land to increase the area of his own land. The farmer would not agree. He was called to the landlord's house. His topknot was tied to his big toe so that he was bent over. (Most Warlis had topknots in those days.) In that stooped position, the beatings were unbearable and *Adivasis* would give in. They agreed to anything and begged to be let go. When this farmer agreed to give up his land, the landlord said, "Now you fall in line! If you do anything like this again, I will kill you."

Another *Adivasi* had refused to go to work. He was hung upside down from a tree and a fire lit under him. Chillies were thrown on the fire and the fumes nearly suffocated him. Then the whipping started. He was let go when he begged in unbearable pain.

Miserable Condition of Women

Women were not spared the ill-treatment meted out by landlords and their supervisors. Landlords treated the wives of the tenant farmers and debtors as their personal property. They firmly believed that the women were theirs to enjoy whenever they desired. They took it as their right sanctified by tradition. It was routine for them to make lewd remarks at the women working for them, brush against them, touch and pinch them, and behave in other sexually aggressive ways. *Adivasis* saw all this and could do nothing. They would say, 'We knew what was happening but did not know what to do." Landlords and forest contractors used *Adivasi* women as sex objects. This was so prevalent that the offspring of non-Hindu landlords, called 'converts', were numerous enough to constitute a community. Add to that the progeny of Hindu landlords from *Adivasi* women.

Mamakwad village lies on the Maharashtra-Gujarat border. It is now a part of Gujarat but was in Bombay province then. We had held a meeting in Mamakwad in the afternoon. The enthusiasm and liveliness of such gatherings was missing here. The village had a mixed population of Dubale and Dhodi communities and Warlis. The proximity of Nargol and Khattalwada villages where landlords ruled had cowed down the farmers. *Adivasis* were afraid in the way grazing cattle is afraid and alert for signs of danger when they sense a tiger nearby.

Comrade Virkar and I stayed overnight in the village thinking the villagers would be more relaxed at night and we could give them courage. But the villagers did not gather to talk as was usual elsewhere. The few who did come were scared and so was the person in whose hut we were staying. We sat talking outside the hut near a fire. Quite late at night, an *Adivasi* couple came to us with a complaint. They had hesitated about whether to approach us and had discussed it with others. They were apprehensive about the consequences. The woman had a four-or five-day-old child with her. The landlord had asked her to report for work on the third day after delivery. When she did not go, she was called to the house on a pretext. Then, with the newborn in her arms, she was slapped repeatedly and abused. She was told to come to work the next day. When she did not go the next day, her husband was beaten. We could not think what should be the immediate response. We could tell them not to perform bonded labour. But the villagers were not united; fear ruled. I talked to the woman and tried to console her. The next day, I took her to the Khattalwad office where we registered a complaint in her name. The complaint did not do more than give her some assurance. With the government officers' connivance, the landlord kept postponing the hearing of the case. No one would give evidence for the woman for fear of the landlord. The woman was in a pitiable state. She had to walk 3-4 miles to Khattalwad carrying her child. From there I would take her to the court in Umbargaon. A part of the journey was on a raft. The landlord was a little scared because of the case. But the woman tired of the long journey to the court and began to miss the hearings. I do not know what happened later.

I was appalled at the idea of a Seth hitting a woman in the face, that too a woman who had delivered a child just four or five days earlier. I was angry at the cowardly farmers. How could their minds be so numb? Why did they not rise up in revolt? I had given them a verbal lashing in my anger. But they heard me out with expressionless faces. The main problem was that, because of the proximity of the landlords' villages, it would need a full-time worker to stay in the area and take on the landlords. Because we did not have such a worker, *Adivasis* did not have the confidence to fight. Because of our activities, landlords would treat them even worse. But since there was no permanent worker there, they would suffer more and more. We then decided not to interfere in that area until we found a worker to station permanently there. Our organisation and movement remained weak in that area and is weak even today.

Adivasis Are as Cattle

The story I heard from a Warli in Kavad village would shock any sensitive human being.

It was the season of sowing paddy. Before planting the rice, the topsoil has to be ploughed and churned to make a knee-deep muddy layer. The softer the muddy layer, the better the crop. The landlords used *Adivasis* as bonded labour for ploughing and planting. Once a farmer called Jethu had the pox. He was running a temperature and could hardly stand. The landlord's assistant went to get him for work. He said, "You better come on your own or I'll drag you there and harness you to the plough." Jethu was frightened and left with the assistant. He knew I was in the village and got away when the assistant was not watching and came to me. He told me that if he did not go to work, he would be harnessed to the plough with a bull on the other side. I could not believe it for a minute. He was saying that he was saved from that fate only because of my presence in the village. He called another villager Jhiper to confirm what he was saying. When I heard Jhiper's story, I realised that, to the landlord there was no difference between a bull and a Warli.

Landlord Nasserwanji's supervisor had ordered Jhiper and some eight to ten others to plough the field to plant paddy. They worked the entire day softening the soil in the field. They did not even have a lunch break. Even a sip of water from a nearby well could be had only when the supervisor was not watching. If the supervisor caught a Warli leaving for a drink of water, he would brandish a stick and shout, "Why didn't you drink water in the morning before coming to work. Bastard, did you ask my permission to leave the field to drink water?" At about seven in the evening, the cattle began to wander out of the field and the supervisor scolded Jhiper to get the cattle back and walk them through the field to make the muddy layer. Jhiper said, "The field is so thorny, how can I walk the cattle through it?" The supervisor complained to the landlord's assistant, who went to the fields to punish the Warli. Jhiper was hitched to a plough with a bull on the other side and made to pull. After a hard day's work, he could barely pull the plough and not pull it well enough for the supervisor. The supervisor began to whip him, drawing blood. Even then, Jhiper ploughed two rounds of the field. Then the secretary rebuked him, "Will you ever be lazy again?" He told other *Adivasis* "Remember what you saw. This will be your punishment, if you don't work."

We talked for long after hearing this story. My hatred for landlords grew manifold. I determined to prepare Warlis to resist and strike back. I could not sleep for a long time that night.

Adivasis were illiterate and did not understand accounts. The landlords maintained the records of all monetary and barter transactions. Whatever amount they said was due, whether truth or lie, was the farmer's debt. If the farmer did not pay, the landlords awarded whatever punishment they could think up. I heard about one such punishment.

A Warli would not pay the debt the landlord claimed was due. He was thrown flat on the ground on his back and a pounding bar was laid across his body. Two men stood on two ends of the bar. They trod on it until the Warli gave in. I had never before heard of such a fiendish form of punishment. I wondered whether these landlords were human or demons.

Landlords did not stop at cruel treatment of *Adivasi* farmers; they went so far as to commit murder. Most landlords had arms licenses and owned guns. They fired in the air to terrorise *Adivasis*. But even if they shot an *Adivasi*, there was no one to hold them accountable. The Seths often threatened, "If you protest, we'll kill you and bury you." The *Adivasis* took this threat seriously because they knew that the landlords could get away with murder, would not have to answer for their deeds. The Adivasi Seva Mandal report of 1945-46 had the following comment on the matter:

1. *A year ago, Adivasis running away due to ill-treatment were pursued by the forest contractor and his men and were fired on. Five persons died and some others were wounded. There is no sign of any action to punish the guilty so far.*
2. *A forest contractor beat two forest clearing workers to death. The contractor was not punished.*

These quotes should be enough to accept the truth of the cases reported by *Adivasis.*

Some middle class people, once they got to know me better and lost some of their prejudices, would say to me in confidence, "How can we talk about these things? These are very influential people. They have even got away with murder. They can kill and dispose of the body and evidence overnight, these pigs." I think there was definitely some truth in what they said.

No Limit to Cruelty

One forest contractor had thrown an *Adivasi* in a coal furnace and burnt him alive. The story is well known in the area.

Adivasis were the main workers who made coal from wood. They had the skill to control the fire to make coal without either burning up the wood or leaving it raw. The key is to watch the fire like a hawk.

Once something went wrong with the furnace and led to a loss for the owner. The owner was so furious that he grabbed an *Adivasi* and threw him into the fire. Many had heard of this incident, but nobody was perturbed by it. I often mentioned it in my speeches. The owners did not hesitate to even burn alive the poor *Adivasis.* This was an atrocity beyond imagining. What could be more inhuman than this?

I heard of an *Adivasi* called Janu whose brother was buried alive. The brother's wife was good looking. Once when Janu had gone to another village, the landlord called the wife to his house.

She guessed why he had called her and refused to go. She was dragged to the house. Nobody dared step forward to help her; they sighed and went back into their huts. They had seen such incidents all their lives. The husband learnt what had happened the next day. He was a spirited man. He gathered together the head of the village, the village elders, and the people of his community and registered his protest. When the landlord heard of it, he had the woman dragged away in front of the husband. The man shouted and fought, but to no avail. In fact, he was punished for protesting; he was buried in a hole in the ground. Janu was threatened not to talk of it or they would break his bones. Janu ran away. The wife, too, ran away. The villagers did not utter a word out of fear. Still, the news spread and a police inquiry was conducted. The case was a farce. The government doctor declared the bones found in the ground to be those of a bull. The landlord was acquitted.

The landlords reduced helpless *Adivasis* to a sub-human state. Without seeing them as animals, landlords could not have treated them as animals. There is no exaggeration in what I have narrated above. Simmington Commission's investigative report bears this out:

> *(b) If they refuse or procrastinate, they are liable to assaults and beatings. These are common occurrences and are usually carried out by the landlords' local agents. I was told on credible authority of men being tied up to posts and whipped. There are also rumours of men in the past having been killed.*
>
> *(f) Landlords will not scruple to use their power in fulfilment of other purpose, for instance, the case of their tenants' womenfolk for the gratification of their lust.*

In the 75 years before 1945, there is no crime in the Indian penal code that the landlords had not committed. In spite of this, there is not a single instance of a landlord or moneylender being punished by law. The question then is how could the atrocities and injustices be allowed? What were the government and its bureaucracy doing? The only answer possible is that, for *Adivasis*, there was no government. Government worked only to protect the exploiting class and help it continue the exploitation and guard its selfish interests. This ugly truth about the government was plain to see.

Exploitative Machinery

No middle class urban person could believe the atrocities and murders that landlords got away with. They felt such things could not happen. Why did no one respond to the crimes until 1945? What were the civil administration and officialdom doing? Was there any such thing as a government? The urbanites thought that there must be some small degree of coercion but the rest must be exaggerated. To convince them, I had to explain the conditions in many different ways.

Even after that, there was only a grudging acknowledgement that maybe it was true, but not belief. But then the conditions were unbelievable. I would also have considered such conditions exaggerated and improbable before I went there. I saw again and again that the government machinery is class-neutral and impartial only within certain limits and in certain conditions.

To maintain their dominance over thousands of *Adivasis*, landlords had two main tools. One was the government bureaucracy and the other was their own supervisors and assistants. These were the crutches on which rested the landlord's exploitation and brutality. They destroyed Warlis' self-esteem and identity. Without the support of government machinery, the private means of oppression would have failed.

Government servants, police personnel, and forest officials at all levels stayed at the landlords' houses when they visited an area. Only officials at higher posts such as district collector, police superintendent, or top forest officers stayed in government guesthouses. In smaller villages, they even stayed in landlords' houses. Landlords looked after them, supplying food and drinks and making their stay comfortable and pleasant. The officials often used landlords' vehicles to travel in the rural areas. Landlords personally looked after the higher officials. For lower posts, they deputed their servants, dependants, assistants, and others.

It was only after the struggle of 1945 that *Adivasis* saw government officials who stayed in a government guesthouse or pitched a tent.

When a new civil or police officer was posted to an area, landlords and forest contractors competed to curry favours with him. These officials usually stayed in the villages where landlords had their homes. Landlords, moneylenders, and forest contractors would buy the officers' gratitude and loyalty by supplying liquor, meat and fish, vegetables, milk, food grains, and other daily needs.

It was October 1945 and the struggle had begun recently in Dahanu. One night I had occasion to spend time at a landlord's home from nine to eleven at night while waiting for the passenger train to Umbargaon. After dinner, he introduced me to the other guests. He introduced one as the Talathi for that area and said the officer was always his guest when he visited the village. Neither he nor the Talathi seemed bothered by this.

Warlis were punished and beaten over minor matters. Kavad village had a dam forming a lake. *Adivasis* worked without wages as bonded labour to build the dam and desilt the lake. After a few days, some *Adivasis* caught a few fish from the lake. Warlis argued that the lake belonged to the village. The landlord claimed the lake and the fish were his property and beat up the *Adivasis*. Not content with that, he filed a case against a hundred *Adivasis*. They were jailed. The case went on for many months. Because of our efforts, the Warlis were at least released on bail. Without that, they would have had to give in and beg the landlord's forgiveness.

This was a regular occurrence. Besides this, government officials facilitated any business the landlord had with their departments. This included raising the farmland rent, allowing false measures, falsifying accounts to show dues from Warlis and recovering those dues, getting Warlis to put their thumb impression on a document, transferring ownership of Warli lands to landlords, and other services for the landlords. Officials greedy for landlords' largesses did all this and worse. They never needed laws or court orders to do this work.

I was staying at Bapgaon once. The district magistrate had stayed at the landlord's home just a little while earlier. On the landlord's orders, Warlis had extracted high-quality, strong liquor from flowers and delivered it to the magistrate. Warlis told me of this. This was how work was done. The government official enjoyed a feast with liquor, exchange of pleasantries, and then siesta at the landlord's house. Then he made the kind of inquiry possible in such circumstances and that too in consultation with the landlord. Sometimes a magistrate just made a notation in a file and left. Under such circumstances, how could *Adivasis* challenge the landlord?

Any protest by Warlis was met with beatings and then court cases that went on until Warlis gave in. Warlis could predict the alarming outcome of a case and stood trembling and speechless in court. They had no hope of getting out on bail. No matter how small the amount of bail, the extremely poor *Adivasis* could not pay it. And nobody would stand surety because of the landlord's pressure. So Warlis would have to remain in lockup. They would not receive meals in the lockup. *Adivasis* feared these conditions. Lawyers were no use to them because they could not afford to pay a lawyer's fee, and the lawyers belonged to the landlords' social and economic class.

The courts and government offices spoke landlords' language because the civil and police administration was on landlords' side. In Umbargaon taluka, one big landlord was an honorary magistrate. He would not even register cases against landlords, leave alone punishing them for locking up, beating, or even raping Warlis. Who would file a criminal case in such an environment? As a Marathi saying goes, when a fence eats into a field, who can protect that field? When the people charged with protecting a population turn into its oppressors, who can protect the victims?

In those days, one could not expect even limited justice. Ordinary people never thought that government officials work for all the people. It was clearly understood that they worked for the rich and powerful. Landlords said quite openly to the protestors, "Who is going to be on your side? All the police, Talathis, magistrates, and courts are on our side. Who will stand up for you? Do what we want and don't complain. Even if we kill you, no one will demand any answers. Do you understand?" They never felt any hesitation or shame in saying this. What they said was true. These rich and powerful people could wax lyrical about the virtues of democracy but practiced harsh autocracy. *Adivasis* had no choice but to meekly accept the atrocities.

This ugly face of the government was starkly visible to *Adivasis*. There was no room for ambiguity. Just as monsoon-winter-summer are natural seasons, so was it natural that government servants would be on landlords' side. They said in their rough language, "What can we do, Madam? Government people eat and drink with the landlords; they do their work. What can we give them? Who will listen to us?"

The forest officers were Warlis' enemies. Warlis were made to clear the jungle, sow seeds, plant saplings, and fight forest fires. Farm work and forest plantation work usually coincided. Warlis had to drop their farm work and go for forest work. The farm work was delayed. But if farmers tried to avoid forest work, the forest officer would compel them to go into the jungle. They had to do this work without any payment. They did not even know that the government paid for this work. They used to say, "We have to do bonded labour for the government in the forest." They knew nothing of the government money sanctioned for the work. It was appropriated by the forest department officials. An *Adivasi* told me that a forest officer had once given them each a fistful of salt for the work done. If *Adivasis* refused to do forest work, forest officers would subject them to all manner of harassment. They would file a barrage of false cases against them. That is why *Adivasis* did any kind of work forest officials gave them without protest.

Whatever the department, government officials never talked to *Adivasis* in a normal tone. Warlis used to tell me that officials would not talk to them except in abusive language. All officials and particularly the police swore at Warlis, manhandled them, and slapped them around; that was the norm. The police and the landlords' supervisors were the most brutal.

Supported by government officialdom was the landlords' private army of supervisors, musclemen, goons, and thugs to subjugate *Adivasis*. These henchmen went from village to village, clubs in hand, terrorising *Adivasis*. The clubs fell on *Adivasis* when the goons saw a reason or when they just felt like it. The women were not spared. This private army was the landlords' means of controlling the villages. They brutalised the population using this machinery and got away with it using the government machinery.

Such was the life of the unprotected, ignorant Warlis who lived in dilapidated huts in small settlements in the jungle. They were not organised and had no support. The community was inert as if dead. They did not even believe that they had the right to live as human beings. All self-respect and pride was gone. Only the landlords' carefully thought-out machinery of exploitation and oppression worked smoothly.

Kochaiwala is the big landlord in Kochai village. His dominance was especially fearsome. He had a Pathan supervisor whom he used for brutal and inhuman treatment of *Adivasis*. When his brutality passed beyond endurance, Comrade Rupaji Kadu led a few *Adivasis* in protest. There was a scuffle and the Pathan was killed. *Adivasis* did not panic. We had reached there, and they drew some comfort from it. Comrade Rupaji made a courageous statement in court, "I was driven by the Pathan's brutality to fight to escape the landlord's vicious grip on my life. I am willing to accept any punishment that is given to me." He was sentenced to seven years rigorous imprisonment. The government had judged him guilty, but the people saw him as their champion and leader. When he was released from jail, *Adivasis* gave him a grand welcome.

After 1945, *Adivasis*' conditions changed. The unity and resolve of *Adivasis* and the leadership of the Communist Party weakened the landlords' means of oppression. We stood by *Adivasis* as supporters of their cause. Kisan Sabha opened offices in the area. *Adivasis*' voice began to be heard in Mumbai. Our lawyers fought their cases free of charge. Cases of crimes against *Adivasis* began to be filed. An organisation grew that could take on the might of landlords. People like Comrade Rupaji, who were ready to sacrifice their lives for their poor brethren, rose to prominence. Warlis began to say that the red flag had come to their rescue like a God.

There was now a check on landlords' and moneylenders' hitherto uncontrolled selfish interests and greed. They began to see us as the enemies of their class. They did all they could to make it impossible for us to work in that area.

V

Our Homes

Our activities put a check on landlords' atrocities and government servants' biased actions. As a consequence, they perceived us as enemies. They tried to make our life impossible and tried all kinds of harassment to get us to leave the area.

I still vividly remember that day. The year was 1954 and Sanyukta Maharashtra Parishad (Federation for United Maharashtra) held a conference about the border question in Shirgaon village in Umbargaon. Shirgaon lay on the Gujarat-Maharashtra border and was known as Seemanagar at that time. Thousands of *Adivasis* attended the conference. Educated urban leaders of all parties in Thane district were present.

The Communist Party was represented on the podium by Comrade Shamrao Parulekar, Comrade Ranadive, and I. The chairperson was DV Potdar. It was the last day of the conference and the thank-you speech was going on. I looked at the mixed crowd of thousands of *Adivasis* and middle-class, educated people, who had come together for one cause. It brought tears to my eyes. I remembered the last eight years of the struggle. I remembered an event in 1945 and was stunned at the difference in conditions between then and now.

I clearly remember that day in May 1945. Only if you understand the happenings of that day can you understand the state of my mind. Since we started a public awareness and education campaign preparatory to the Zari conference, false propaganda against us had begun. Civil servants and police officers aided it and the landlord class brought to bear their enormous clout.

Once we had a rally in Talwada village on market day. On the way back from the rally, we met Comrade Redkar who was a teacher in Nargol village and had attended the rally because it was a school holiday.

Comrade Dalvi and I had been going from village to village. We had not had a decent meal for days and had not had a bath for three or four days. I had not even combed my hair. We thought, before continuing on, we would have a tea, find somewhere to take a bath, and have a meal. Shirgaon was landlords' village. We thought we would get good food there and also because we had never been to that village, we decided to go to Shirgaon.

Another reason to go to Shirgaon was to spend the day there when we were free. Since all the farmers worked as bonded labour all day long, our meetings happened at night. That left the day free to explore Shirgaon.

Ganapati Temple

We walked from Talwad to Bhilad station. We could not face a further three-mile walk to Shirgaon. *Tongas* would appear near the station when a train was due, which was some time later. We decided to wait. In those days, there were no tea shops and restaurants as there are today. There was a small homely hotel on the road to Shirgaon. We got water there to wash our faces. We had tea to our heart's content though not to the satisfaction of our taste buds. As the train time neared, people started arriving at the station. *Tongas* started to appear. My hair was not combed and not oiled. My clothes were dusty. It was summer and I went without washing or bathing for two days at a time. The landlords and middle-class people at the station cast meaningful glances at us as if to say they knew who we were and looked at us with immense contempt and hatred, nudging, gesturing and talking to one another. We ignored them. There was no point in paying attention. The three of us engaged a *tonga* and started for Shirgaon.

As our *tonga* came to Shirgaon village, the village began to move as in an earthquake. Some half-closed the doors and from behind the doors, looked out at us and pointed at us as if saying "Look, it's them; they have come to our village." Men, women, and children rushed out onto their verandas to see us and gave shouts to gather others. Some stood on the side of the road while others gathered in the village square. They were curious. We had gone there for the first time and were not sure of where to go and what to do. The *tonga* driver asked where he should take us and we could not tell him. I guessed that there would be a temple in the village and I asked him to take us to the Ganapati temple. He took us there and we went into the temple.

The temple had steps going up to a veranda and a cement bench on the veranda to the right of the steps. We put down our luggage on the bench. We wanted to stay there until the evening. I went around to the back to see if there was a well. A young man called Pimputkar came over. He was probably the temple priest. He told me that we could not stay in the temple because the village *Panch* was opposed to it. He asked us to leave. We were wondering what to do in these difficult circumstances. We did not know any Warli in the village. And the white collar establishment would not let us stay in the temple. The *tonga* had left and we were dying to have a bath. We could not think what to do. I firmly told the priest, "No matter what the *Panch* says, we will stay here. You say that the *Panch* objects. All right. Call a meeting of all the villagers. Let's see if the people of this village tell us to go." The boy walked off muttering angrily. We decided to spend the day in Shirgaon. We were new to the village and the landlords were spoiling for a fight. So we thought we would look around the village and move out of the temple if we found somewhere else. We were expecting to find a welcome in some nearby *Adivasi* village.

Comrade Dalvi and I went out to make arrangements. In a little while, Comrade Dalvi came back having made arrangements for baths at a blacksmith's well. In answer to his request, the blacksmith had said, "You are not going to take away my well. You are welcome to use it for a bath. I have no objection." We went to the blacksmith's house for a bath. Comrade Dalvi drew a bucket of water from the well and I began to soap the clothes. He dropped the bucket into the well again, and just then a woman came yelling out of the house, "Why have you come to our well? Don't take water from my well. If you want to take a bath, go to the public well on the road. Pick up your things and get out of here." She only just stopped short of throwing away our clothes. After this, there was no hope of a bath! We realised that a threatening message from some important village personage had caused the change in attitude. We picked up our clothes and returned to the temple. I cannot describe how we felt at that moment.

We now became adamant. I went out to find some other place. There was a Muslim bangle-maker, who lived just outside the village. Hers was an independent business. She welcomed us into her home with affection. She had a bathroom and I finally had a bath and washed off the dust. I felt better and thanked the woman for her kindness. I returned to the temple. Comrade Dalvi had had a bath at the public well. Comrade Redkar was sitting on the bench where we had left our luggage. Baths accomplished, we wanted to see about lunch. The village had some conveniences but not a lunch home. Comrade Dalvi went to the *Adivasis* at Andherpada to make arrangements for lunch.

Comrade Redkar sent messages to some of his students in Shirgaon. Some of them showed the gumption and affection to come to see him at the temple. But most did not have the courage for it. They gave lame excuses such as "My aunt is not well," or "Nobody is at home." Some said plainly, "There is opposition at home. We cannot come." We understood the students could not help and waited for Comrade Dalvi.

Shelter at Andherpada

Comrade Dalvi returned having made arrangements in an *Adivasi* home at Andherpada. We bought some snacks from a hotel in the village. Then we picked up our luggage and went to Andherpada. We had never met the *Adivasi* before, but he gave us some water and, with a great deal of hesitation, asked us whether we would sit down to lunch. He thought we were important people and would not eat in his home. When he realised that we were there particularly for lunch, he was glad. The women of his family had threshed some paddy, cleaned the rice, and put it on the fire to cook. It was one o'clock in the afternoon when we reached Andherpada and we were very hungry. We asked them to cook only rice. We had brought some *bhajia*, which we ate with the rice. Our host sat against the wall smoking a *bidi*. We had a long talk with him as we ate. We learnt a good deal. He was happy that our manner was easy and open with him. We told him about the conference at Zari. We described our reception in Shirgaon. When he heard the story, he warmed to us.

At around three in the afternoon, I was lying down to rest outside the hut. Comrade Dalvi and Redkar were resting on a cot near there. None of us slept. We talked while resting. We planned to start for the meeting at Bhilad after around five in the evening when the sun began to go down. Just then, landlord Arekar came calling loudly, "Is anybody at home?" We did not answer. He sat down on the cot and said to us, "That Pimputkar is just a kid. He doesn't know anything. He told you some nonsense. Please come to the village now and take some tea before you go on." We were surprised at this transformation in just three or four hours. We learnt the reason for the change later.

After we left for Andherpada, some village leaders gathered to deliberate the incident. They thought that what had happened was not right. They did not feel remorse that a respectable woman was not allowed to even take a bath in the village and was thrown out. About that, they had the boastful feeling: "We didn't let them stay in our village. We drove them out." The change in attitude was forced by self-interest. The landlords lived in close proximity to *Adivasis*. They spent a lot of time in the jungle with *Adivasis* for farming and on other business. They worried about the consequences if *Adivasis* turned hostile. That is why they sent Arekar to invite us. We flatly refused to do so. *Adivasis* did not form any right or wrong interpretation of it.

We spelt out certain points to Arekar quite clearly. We described the atrocities committed by landlords and the exploitation of the helpless Warlis. We made it clear that we knew the treatment we received in Shirgaon was a part of an effort to stop our struggle. The man was firm about what he wanted. He ignored all our arguments and instead preached to us, "Social workers have always had to face such agonies, insults, and hardships. Did Agarkar suffer any less anguish? He had to suffer slights." We were amused to hear him pontificate. We declared that the days of the landlords' oppressive rule were coming to an end. So saying, we left together. Comrade Redkar went to Nargol, Arekar to Shirgaon, and Comrade Dalvi and I to Bhilad.

We had only gone a little way when we wondered if the village bigwigs would go to Andherpada and abuse the Warli family for sheltering us, maybe even beat them up. If this sapped the Warlis' will and courage, it would have a negative impact on our message and the Zari conference. We had to coach the *Adivasis* in how to respond if the landlord threatened them. Comrade Dalvi went back to Andherpada to give instructions to the Warlis.

I sat on a rock to wait for Comrade Dalvi to return. When he returned, he seemed quite encouraged. The Warlis were very pleased that we had admonished a landlord's messenger about ill-treatment of Warlis in front of a Warli family. It was a novelty to them that we had stood up to the landlord and had given him a verbal lashing. They had sent a message: "Tell Madam that whatever happens, even if we are killed, we will not give in to fear." They had never heard anyone speak to the landlord in such a manner. This was a new experience in their lives. We had given voice to their thoughts and feelings. We too had the new awareness of this state of mind in Warlis. We were very happy and started once again on the road to Bhilad.

For many days after we left, our stay in Shirgaon was the main topic of conversation among Warlis and landlords alike. Both sides watched with keen interest where we went next and what we did.

Let Bygones Be Bygones

It was inevitable that I would remember the day I spent in Shirgaon in 1945 as I sat on the conference podium in 1954. A great deal had happened between 1945 and 1954. In 1953, when I first went to Shirgaon for preliminary discussions about the United Maharashtra Federation, Bhalyamama Khadapekar said right at the outset, "What flowed was the Ganga and what remains is the sanctified water. Let us forget what happened in the past and start afresh." I made a suitable reply. The meeting was conducted in a friendly atmosphere. I stayed at Nilubhau Arekar's home that day. From that day to today, whenever I visit Shirgaon, I stay at his home. His wife Leelatai Arekar, his elder brother Tatyasaheb Arekar, and his two children treat me like a member of the family.

The Arekar family has nothing to do with any political matter except the demand for a United Maharashtra and especially the inclusion in Maharashtra of the 16 Marathi-majority villages in Umbargaon taluka, which were then included in Gujarat. Despite their apolitical attitudes, the Congress government harassed the Arekar family for the affectionate and humane treatment they gave me. They had to suffer the displeasure of the government and economic losses. Their licensed gun kept for protection in the jungle was taken away. These things were painful and insulting, but Nilubhau Arekar did not let them depress him. He did not abandon his humane values. Since 1954, most of the middle-class, white collar people in Shirgaon have treated me well.

In the village that had refused me a single drop of water, in 1954 I stood on a podium and received a bouquet of flowers. Gratitude for the people's struggle that had made this possible brought tears to my eyes.

Tree Trunk

Back in 1945, we held a rally in Khattalwad, which was a village dominated by landlords. Not many *Adivasis* came to the rally. They had not yet developed the courage to openly attend a rally. There was not much to be gained from holding a rally there, but it brought a lot of trouble. But word spread that, right in the stronghold of the landlords, there had been harsh denunciation of their atrocities. It had a positive effect on Warlis.

In Khattalwad, there was a person called Antaji Kale who was a devoted follower of Lokmanya Tilak and had worked in his Paisa Fund movement. He attended our rally.

In Khattalwad, the chief police official—the Police Patil—was one Virkar who was related to the landlord family of Pimputkar. The Pimputkar household had no male member acting as the head of the family. The family's position of village Patil was held by the widow who was the head of the family. She was known in the area as *Salu Patleen*. Her brother Virkar performed the duties of the Patil on her behalf. He was the uncrowned king of the backward village. He wore rings on all four fingers and went around the village swinging a stick in his hand and terrorising the poor. Virkar had come to our rally to write down the speeches. Our speeches made him furious. The rally raised the temperature in the village. Virkar stormed around like a wild animal. Discussions and strategy meetings were held on the landlords' spacious verandas about how to destroy us. Our politics, our terminology, our speeches—all were new to this village. No one had welcomed us before the rally. What was the chance that anyone would welcome us afterwards?

Antaji Kale's son had a hotel in Khattalwad. It was partitioned with a curtain. The front was a hotel and the back was vacant. Kale boasted that he was not afraid of anybody and would have us stay in his hotel. He gave us the vacant half at the back. Villagers came and looked at us, some with curiosity and others with derision. Nobody tried to talk to us.

When Antaji Kale learnt of this, he had his wife invite us to lunch at his home. I was a little surprised. I found out later that Kale was eccentric and hot-headed. He did not get along with anyone in the village, and people stayed away from him.

During the Paisa Fund movement, Kale had visited my father, Laxman Raghunath Gokhale, who had donated 250 rupees. Kale still remembered this. When Mrs Kale invited me, I accepted with alacrity because I had a problem arranging meals and a bath.

The women of the house treated me with kindness. Kale was sitting outside and did not come in at all. I had my lunch and went back to the hotel. I wrote a little and then left on my propaganda tour. I was going for just two days and took only the necessities with me and left the rest of the luggage in the hotel.

When I returned after two days, the atmosphere had changed. The Patil had gone around the village with a gun and a stick in hand and threatened everyone. Kale's son had lost his nerve. Virkar had given a strict warning, "Don't you dare shelter these people!

I will beat the hell out of you. I won't let you so much as step into this village ever again." He had the backing of the landlord. No one had the courage to oppose him and shelter me. People just stared at me in helplessness.

Khattalwad was just like Shirgaon. It was getting on to evening and I was sitting under a tree outside Kale's hotel with my luggage. I was alone, and it would soon be evening. What should I do? Where could I go? I marvelled at how the human mind worked. The hotel was locked. What was the point of sitting under a tree in front of the locked hotel? But Kale had once given me shelter and I did not want to go away. I decided to remain under the tree. Evening came and I still had no shelter, leave alone a bed for the night. I started walking to Sanjan station thinking that I would sleep in the waiting room. But soon I had another thought. Sanjan station was about three miles away and I was alone. Village streets are deserted once night falls. It was not safe for me to walk alone to the station. So I turned back. It was night when I returned to Khattalwad. The village was silent and nothing moved. The shops had closed. The landlords' homes were closed up for the night. They must have assumed that I had gone to stay with some Warli as in Shirgaon. There was no electricity in the village. Even the gaslights in shops were no longer lit. I thought that Virkar and his gang must be fast asleep after a big meal and liquor. They would not come out again that night. In those days, there was no taboo against landlords drinking toddy and liquor.

I again arrived in front of Kale's hotel. Where else could I go in the night? I did not know where the Warli settlements were. I tied my luggage in a bundle, put it under a tree, and sat on it. I covered myself with a sheet. I had no choice but to spend the night sitting under the tree. The slightest noise frightened me, made me tremble. Every moment seemed like an eon. The thought of spending the entire night under the tree made me numb. Time stood still.

Just then, a man came out of a nearby hut. He saw me and came over. I was frightened at first. But he was a poor, harmless man. He had a small tea shop in his home. He came to me and said, "Madam, what can I do? I cannot take on the people I must live among. I live in this village and can't afford to oppose the big shots." He brought me tea in a small loti. In those circumstances, I needed the tea and drank it greedily. He told me, "You can sit or sleep here without any worry. We are close by. This place is safe." He said this and left. In a little while, three or four *Adivasis* arrived. They lit fires and stayed with me all night. They told me that I could sleep. Warlis knew the details of my whereabouts at all times. How they found out I would never know. They did not let on, but they watched my movements. Whenever I needed help, they would appear unexpectedly, as if by magic. Their loyalty swept away my mental and physical fatigue in a moment. My heart filled with gratitude. I spent the night under the tree with the *Adivasis*. They left at dawn and I went to the hotel to wash and have some tea.

I was dawdling near the hotel before leaving for the next rally, thinking about the happenings of the previous day. Just then Antaji Kale came there and told me that some rabble-rousers in the village had misled his wife about me. They had told her, "The woman you received in your home and sat down to lunch with eats with Warlis. She does not respect any religious practices nor believes in God. She has married a Saraswat." This had led to a mighty row between husband and wife and Kale had gone without food for two days. His wife believed that her home was defiled because I ate there with her. She was a traditional, God-fearing, religious woman. She calmed down only after a lot of arguments and purification of the house by sprinkling cow's urine, during which two days Kale observed an unintended fast.

Kale told me this story. He was crestfallen as he expressed his inability to invite me to his home again. I felt bad on hearing this. I asked him, "If things were so bad, why did you invite me? Your home unnecessarily suffered a quarrel. I would have managed somehow." I tried to make Kale feel better. He answered "No problem. Once I had invited Maharshi Karve to my home for lunch. Some people in the village had created an uproar in the same way. These things happen." As we talked, an insurance agent by the name of Karhadkar came along. Kale introduced us. At Karhadkar's wife's insistence, I would stay at their home for a long time afterwards. Whatever his reasons, the family welcomed me with kindness for many years.

Court Building and Hall

The situation in Dahanu was similar to that in Umbargaon. There was no place available to set up an office, hold a meeting, or organise a rally. All the places belonged to landlords. The movement grew rapidly in Dahanu taluka. Landlords and tenant farmers filed many complaints against each other. Landlords had lawyers from their own socioeconomic class to represent them. *Adivasis* could not find lawyers who would work for the amount they could afford to pay. Our party had full-time workers who received a monthly salary and decided to make a similar arrangement for legal work. We requested the Thane lawyer Bhadkamkar to represent the farmers. He agreed to do so at a small wage. We procured with great difficulty a room for his office. It was a small room in a corner of one Phatak's bungalow and was close to the district magistrate's court. Hundreds of farmers began to go to him. To have their own lawyer in Dahanu had a positive impact on them. But Bhadkamkar suffered from asthma and the damp air of Dahanu was bad for his health. He had to leave Dahanu.

We later did not have the use of the room we had rented for the lawyer. We had filed a case on behalf of a farmer Nanhu Bendu Gharat against the landlords Barjor Seth and Sugandhi Seth and the police officer Salvi. It was a notable case at that time. The district collector Bedekar, Comrade Parulekar, and I were to testify in the case. We and some workers went to Dahanu to attend court. Bhadkamkar was not in Dahanu, but because he was the party's official lawyer, we went to his room. But we had to vacate the room in just two days.

That room was very small. There was a small room, a veranda, and a common well for the entire house. I always had a problem about having a bath. I spent one day without a bath. The next day, I received permission to bathe in the bathroom next to the well. I had never drawn water from a well before. This was the first time that I would draw water from a well and bathe in it. When I began to draw water, the middle class women of the house looked at me with amusement and smiled. I became self-conscious. I felt sorry for myself. I thought that had I been a Congress party worker or a woman's activist, or just a tourist, these women would have welcomed me with open hearts. They would have given me hot water for a bath and insisted that I had lunch with them. They would have accepted me as one of them and would have helped me in many ways! I pitied their self-satisfaction. Why did they not want to talk to me about my work, my aims, and their good or bad consequences? Why were they so apathetic? Or did they fear me? Their attitude reflected the class hatred that grew out of their middle class values. I was disgusted at their narrow lives. Unconsciously, I compared them to the *Adivasi* women I knew. *Adivasi* women who, in spite of their troubles, worked hard and enjoyed a free life seemed to me more capable. I finished my bath and returned to the room thinking such thoughts.

Many *Adivasis* had brought their complaints to the office. By the time we had finished their work and got up to arrange our evening meal, it was late afternoon. A lawyer from Thane and his wife came to the office. He told us, "This room belongs to Bhadkamkar. We have spoken to him about using it. Please vacate this room right away." With the connivance of the owner of the house, they had come to throw us out. They spoke to us in an overbearing manner as a landlord would speak to a tenant who was not paying rent. None of us said anything. I said, "I am a woman. Where can I go at this time of the night?" But this did not have any effect on them. The wife seemed to be very angry. She would not listen to anything and kept up a chant of "vacate this room immediately". We could have said that we would not move without a letter from Bhadkamkar. But our people were proud.

Comrade Parulekar said we would sleep under a tree but not in that room. Comrade Virkar declared that we would not stay there another minute. He started bringing out our luggage. We also considered that we had a lot of important work and should not waste energy fighting such petty people. We had only a little luggage, which we assembled in the courtyard. Just then our lawyer Godiwala arrived; he was to appear in the hearing scheduled for the next day.

We faced the big question of where so many people would go? On the way from Dahanu to the station, there was a banyan tree. It had the customary stone platform around the base of the trunk. If all else failed, we would stay there for the night.

By a coincidence, Yamunabai Phatak, sister to Comrade Nagarkar, was visiting a home near the bungalow from which we had been evicted. I went to her and asked where we could stay the night. She immediately replied, "What's so difficult about that! Where would you go at this time? You can sleep here on this clean, tiled veranda. You can make other arrangements in the morning." We took our luggage to the veranda and slept there. She had had the veranda swept and provided drinking water. In those days, Nanasaheb Phatak and his wife Yamunabai lived near Dahanu station. I often stayed in their house. The family treated me with kindness. As the movement grew and many farmers began to visit, I stopped staying with them. But their doors were always open to me. We have close and friendly relations even today.

We had to make some living arrangements the next day. How could we pass two days on the veranda? At nine o'clock the next morning, I met the judge Hakim. I told him that we needed to be in Dahanu to testify but had problems finding a place to stay. Hakim immediately made arrangement for us. The courthouse was a spacious building near the sea. He gave us a large room in it. It was a fine arrangement. There was a big rug in the room. The *Adivasi* caretaker of the court, who lived in a hut nearby, looked after our meals and tea. We spent a pleasant two days in that large room refreshed by the lovely sea breeze.

Once the hearing of the case started, the court would be packed with people. The news that we had been given a room in the courthouse spread like fire. In a small village, this became a topic of discussion. Some were angry and others curious about us. We rose in some people's esteem because the court had made the arrangements. Once our work was done, we thanked the judge and left. Our lawyer Godiwala and Comrade Parulekar left for Mumbai. We went to the villages to continue our work.

Horse Stable

Whenever we went to Dahanu court, it meant a long wait in the court, and we were reluctant to walk a long distance to a village. We needed a place in Dahanu where we could meet *Adivasis*. But the big landlords owned most of the places. Who would give us a place? We started making inquiries among the poor people. But the landlords threatened them. The only kind of person who could give us a place would be someone of independent attitude, running an independent business, and not attracting anybody's attention. Babu Tangewala was one such person. He gave us space in his horses' stable. This was located at one end of the village near the bay and close to the district magistrate's court. The hut was approximately 20 feet by 16 feet. It was partitioned to make a room of about 8 feet by 16 feet, where Babu lived with his wife and children. The other part was further divided by a partition made of sticks lashed together but not cemented and smoothed with mud. In one part were Babu's horses and in the other our office. The place had no door, but what could one expect in a stable. Babu told us that he could not make any improvements and that we should take the place only if we liked it as it was. For us, there was no question of likes or dislikes.

We were content that we got a place for an office, no matter what it was like. I had the usual problem of having a bath. There was a boulder behind the stable and I took baths there in the evenings. It was possible because the place was not frequented in the evenings.

We used to take tea in the hotel and eat snacks like chivada instead of lunch. The junk food we ate all day did not satisfy our hunger and at night we ate rice with dal or vegetables. It was easier to cook a proper meal in the evening. The *Adivasis* who came to our office for court matters sometimes spent the night there.

When we returned from the courts, they would get busy arranging three stones, lighting a fire, and cooking rice for dinner. Our meals were cooked together and eaten together. They understood our difficulties and solved them. They brought two earthen pots to store drinking water. They got banana leaves for plates. Later they made a lot of plates of leaves tacked together. They cooked the dal rice in an earthen pot. We enjoyed those meals. It brought home to us how simple things like earthen pots and pans could solve problems and make life easy.

In the stable in the light of the cooking fire, we sat talking late into the night about the *Adivasis*' lives, the events in the villages, and news from the Dahanu landlords' camp. We all slept in the stable. One thing still gives me goose bumps when I remember it. When there was a strong wind, it blew dust and dried horse droppings, making a dirty layer on the rice if we happened to be eating at the time. We would remove the top layer of the rice and try to quickly eat the rest. There was nothing else to do. I used to sleep on a small rug with a thin sheet drawn over my head. The horses' neighs disturbed my sleep. A gust of wind would cover us in dust and dried droppings. In the morning, the Warlis would sweep the stable and then leave. Other Warlis came for their court matters. Since there was no other place available, we had to spend some days in such conditions in the stable.

I wonder how I lived, and happily, through those days—I who had lived on the third floor of a four storied house in Pune, in my own clean and airy room, falling asleep while reading in a bed with two mattresses.

It was surprising that Babu gave us this place in defiance of any potential opposition. He did not take rent. We were not getting a place, and he could easily have demanded rent. That he did not do so shows the large-heartedness of this poor man. His *tonga* was kept outside the hut. He worked all day long. We never knew when he returned at night and when he left in the morning. His wife avoided us. She was afraid of what the neighbours would think.

Also, she did not like the fact that Babu had given us the place without charging rent. His economic condition has improved a great deal now. I remember the old days when I first knew him. Today, he has built a house. During the struggle when thousands of Warli were in Dahunu jail, Babu had the contract to provide them meals. He earned well on that. He says even today that he has the righteousness of the struggle to thank for his improved condition.

Powerful people often argue that whatever be one's political opinions, one can maintain good personal relationships. But they did not act on this professed belief. They did all they could to make things impossible for us. But that did not stop us. The force of the movement burst all dams and surged ahead.

Patil's Bungalow

While we were staying in the stable, we were looking for another place. After a few days, we got a place in a village functionary's house near Babu's hut. The monthly rent was 5 rupees. This was our office until November 21, 1946, when the government expelled us from Thane district.

Comrade Kama Ranadive was the full-time worker in this area and lived and worked in this office. The place was very small and inconvenient. It was said that the house had been a lock-up in the old days. We had a small room on the first floor. The staircase going to the room was pitch-dark. The first floor had a small square landing and rooms all around. This architecture made it easy to believe that it had been used as a lock-up. Ours was a corner room about eight feet by eight feet with a door and a window. The first floor was not tiled but was laid with wooden planks. We made only tea in the room and went out for lunch. Water had to be brought up from the well. The room did not have a basin. We would wash our hands and dishes in a large vessel and then throw the water out of the window. The bungalow did not have toilets. In the morning when cooking fires were lit, smoke filled the room and set eyes and noses streaming. We could still console ourselves that we at least had a place to lie down and sleep. But the nights passed in restlessness. The wooden floor had innumerable bedbugs. If one lit a torch at night, one would see bedbugs crawling over the bed like pockmarks on a person's face. Comrade Kama and I each wrapped a sheet covering the entire body and sat up the entire night with the light on. In the morning, we learnt that all the homes were similarly infested. People were used to it and did not mind. We tried using insecticides. But the entire house was infested; the insecticide was ineffectual. Soon we got used to it. Unless one experiences it, one can't imagine what kinds of things a person can become habituated to. There was a bathroom in the adjacent room. But lack of a toilet was a big problem. The men and women there went to the bay early in the morning to relieve themselves. Comrade Ranadive and other colleagues began to do the same thing. For me, this was a big problem.

One Dandekar lived nearby and on his property there was a makeshift toilet with sackcloth supplementing sticks and mud walls. A young man related to Dandekar often came to us and discussed political issues. When he saw my problem, he told me I could use that toilet and he took me there. A big problem was solved and I was deeply grateful to the young man. But the arrangement proved to be short-lived. I benefited from the young man's civility for only two days. On the third day, with great reluctance, he told me, "My family is opposed to it. I am helpless." Once again we saw how people of the exploiting class became devoid of humanity when class struggle intensified. I saw this again and again during the movement. We had to face difficulties and troubles, deal with them no matter how, and carry on our work.

There was one gain from landlords' opposition. As their opposition grew harsher, *Adivasis*' confidence in us grew stronger.

Our office remained in that house until November 1946 when we were banished from the area. It did not look imposing as an office. It was not on the main road and did not have a sign. We ate and lived in the same room that was the office. There was neither a chair nor a table. All it had was a rug and a small trunk. Big landlords were forced to come to this humble office during the resistance when *Adivasis* demanded 'the permit from the red flag' before they would start the work of cutting grass. This office was a pillar of strength for *Adivasis*. Government spies loitering around to watch it also made it important. The people's will made that small room in an old house on the fringes of a village a busy centre of activity. From this office we issued the instruction to strike work cutting wood in the jungle. *Adivasis* often told landlords: "Covering the cock to stop it crowing cannot prevent the sun rising." It was so true. (Pushing the office into poor accommodation did not prevent it from becoming powerful.)

The landlords' opposition proved to be ineffective. Bonded labour was abolished and Warlis began to get wages for farm work. Debtors who had borrowed for marriage expenses were set free. Rent payment in grain was abolished. Rent was fixed in monetary terms and at five times the land tax. Land prices were fixed. A law was passed that any farmer who could pay the price of land in twelve instalments would become the owner of the land. These concessions were won at the cost of deep wounds to *Adivasis*.

VI

Death to Bonded Labour

The Maharashtra unit of the Kisan Sabha had held a convention in Titwala, which Comrade Govind Devdekar attended with 25-30 Warlis. The reception at the convention surprised the Warlis, who had always been treated with contempt by the educated middle class. They were received with great warmth and affection. It awakened their pride and self-esteem.

Some ten thousand farmers attended the convention. The Warli attendees had never seen such a big meeting of farmers. It made a great impact on them. They appreciated the power of unity. Warlis used to be afraid of educated classes and rarely spoke before them. But the convention had such an impact that a Warli got up unprompted and asked to make a speech after the resolution to abolish bonded labour was placed before the assembly. He presented the Warlis' arguments and feelings against bonded labour with strong feeling. He was a little nervous, but spoke firmly. The suppressed sentiments of many years had breached the dams and burst forth in speech. His speech was very effective. He reported that, before the rains, Warlis had to abandon their own fields and work the landlord's farms. The landlord forced them to prepare his own land for sowing. As a result, the Warlis' rice crop suffered and the yield was poor. Yet the same landlord said to the Warli, "Look at the crop on my land. Yours' is not as good because you are lazy; you don't want to work hard."

The Warli attendee said in his speech: "The landlords used Warlis' carts without any payment. All the members of a family were put to work—one in the jungle, another at home, and yet another somewhere else . . . From now on, Warlis will not do bonded labour nor accept any beatings."

We did not realise then how deep an impact the Titwala convention made on *Adivasis.*

The *Adivasis* left the convention carrying red flags. They saw the red flag as their friend and guide. The Warlis who returned from the convention were not the same people as before. They were transformed. They had lost fear. On their own initiative, they handed over their routine work to others and went from village to village, red flag in hand, spreading the message of the convention. The call to abolish bonded labour that energised the Warli community resounded in the jungle.

Warlis did not see the resolution as just words on paper meant merely to express good intentions. To them, the resolution was a solemn oath to implement the change without delay, and so they went to work.

What was the system of bonded labour? It was a system of terrible exploitation. Under this system, landlords and moneylenders could make *Adivasis* do all the physically demanding work without paying a paisa, for just a handful of coarse rice. The landlords could demand work at any time. If the bonded labourers refused or tried to avoid work, they would be beaten. There were stories of even murders.

When the landlord gave a piece of land to an *Adivasi* for cultivation, he set a part as *khand* or his share. The measurement of the *khand* was often distorted by tampering with weights. The landlord did not spend so much as a rupee on raising the crop of which he claimed a share. He also took a share of subsidiary crops like pulses. If the farmer did not give a share of these, the landlord took a larger share of the rice. If the Warli grew vegetables, he had to give them to the landlord. If the farmer kept chicken, Parsi and Muslim landlords took the chicken and eggs. During the monsoon, the landlords demanded the *kartool* (or *kantoli*) vegetable. *Adivasis* spent hours in the jungle searching for this vegetable. If they could not give it, they had to give a larger share of the rice produce.

When the roofs of the landlords' houses were to be thatched, they sent a message to the bonded labourers. Warlis had to respond immediately to the summons and do the work without payment. When the landlord needed wood, *Adivasis* had to chop the wood, cart it to the landlords' house, and neatly stack it there. Nothing was paid either for the carts or for the labour. If the landlord wanted leaf plates or leaves for *bidis*, *Adivasis* had to gather and clean the leaves and make the plates. They had to chop and clean the sticks used for brushing teeth and deliver them in neat bundles. If they did not do any of this, they had to give a larger share of the rice crop to the landlord or suffer a beating.

This was not all. Bonded labourers were made to do all the work related to farming—building and repairing dams, preparing the soil, ploughing and sowing, weeding, and reaping —all compulsory and all without payment, and a priority over the labourer's own farm. They had to keep working until all the paddy was gathered and stored in the landlord's godowns.

Landlords had two places of residence. That forced *Adivasis* to walk 10 miles and more to deliver eggs and vegetables, besides looking after the cattle and poultry. Warlis walked 10-15 miles with big loads strapped to their backs. They often told me, "Madam, the load was so heavy that we could not even scratch the back if it itched." Their backs and hands would be numb from balancing the load.

Landlords were not satisfied even when all their needs were met. They took advantage of the Warlis' ignorance and helplessness to use bonded labour to build their bungalows and big houses.

Warlis told us that they had built the roads to the landlords' houses in Vankas and in Kochai as bonded labour without any payment. They built the embankment to the lake in Kavad. They built the bridge in Kochai. These houses, roads, and bridges, built without paying wages, made landlords seem like the knights and potentates of history. Landlords had filled their homes with thousands of such comforts built for free by Warlis and had amassed great wealth. There was no work that they did not make Warlis do. The bonded labourer was no better than a slave. They were not referred to by name but were called *vethya*, meaning bonded labourer. Any refusal or delay was punished with whips and blows. This was how landlords had sucked the vitality out of *Adivasis*' lives. Their lives were bloodied as if scored by a tiger's claws.

As soon as Warlis resolved to stop bonded labour, landlords brought out their weapons. It was necessary to organise Warlis on a large scale to meet the landlords' challenge. To this end, we organised a farmers' convention in Zari in Umbargoan taluka on May 23, 1945. Five thousand *Adivasis*, including five hundred women, attended the convention. This level of participation was the fruit of the work Comrade Dalvi and I had done, going from village to village and developing affection, confidence, and awareness amongst Warlis.

Comrade Parulekar's speech in this convention was very effective. He made an effort to use simple language. His personality was such that, when he stood up and began to speak in a strong but deep voice, the audience would be electrified. His speech left a deep impression. Warlis went back to their villages with a new energy, raising slogans to abolish bonded labour. Many Warlis hung around Comrade Parulekar for a long time after the speech.

After this convention, the collective resistance to the system of bonded labour began. Those who tried to cause a rift in the ranks were boycotted. Those who were afraid gained confidence. The Warli resistance spread so rapidly through the jungle that within three weeks, the centuries-old tradition of bonded labour was consigned to the garbage dump of history.

As soon as Warlis stopped bonded labour, landlords declared that they would not give *Khavti*. *Khavti* was the grain landlords lent to Warlis towards the end of the agricultural year, when the Warlis' small stock of food grains was depleted. That stock was small enough to begin with considering how much they gave as the landlords' share. The borrowed food grain was repaid at the rate of one and a half, two, or three times the original. Some landlords gave a sack of rice and, just six months later, took three sacks of rice in repayment. This interest rate was sheer robbery. But if landlords did not give *Khavti*, *Adivasis* would starve.

Warlis were not cowed down by landlords' threats to withhold *Khavti*. They were determined that they would eat roots and leaves or even accept starvation death but not do bonded labour, not surrender to the mighty. Landlords needed workers on their fields and did not want to give up the huge interest on *Khavti*. Their words turned out to be empty threats.

Warlis' boycott of defectors was rather strict. They tied bones to the hut of the person to be boycotted. The bones signified that the person has been excommunicated. Not only did all transactions with the person stop, but no one would take even a drink of water in his hut. We put a stop to this practice. It was one thing to suspend social ties with a person for a short period and quite another to permanently cut him off from the community. Since they were all backward, it was better to explain and persuade than to excommunicate a person.

In the farming season following the Zari convention in May, *Adivasis* refused to work for free on the strength of their collective force. Landlords were forced to pay wages for work.

After the success of the resistance in Umbargaon, we planned to strengthen the organisation and activities there and then move on to Dahanu taluka. But *Adivasis* had a different plan.

Some *Adivasis* from Dahanu had heard about the Zari convention and had come there to find out what the 'red flag' was all about. They knew that the red flag would defeat landlords. When they heard of the success of the Umbargaon resistance, they did not wait any longer and rushed into an uprising. They carried the red flag from village to village and organised rallies. As many as two thousand people attended these rallies. They repeated the slogans from the Zari convention; they did not know anything else. Farmers were so impatient to throw off the yoke of brutality, bonded labour, oppression, and beating that soon eight to ten thousand people were attending the rallies. Warlis then felt the need of speakers and began to send me urgent and peremptory messages to my home in Kalyan. (I lived in Kalyan at that time.) "The rally is on such and such a date. It is the command of the red flag that you come immediately to make a speech." These orders often arrived late and I could not go. But their movement went ahead, and fast. The *Bombay Chronicle* of October 22, 1945 had the following.

The *Adivasis* who were tame and docile till this day suddenly became class conscious and they began to collect in large numbers under the Red Flag. Mass meetings were held throughout these talukas. People marched miles and miles to attend meetings. They carry sticks in their hands. Their enthusiasm appeared to be unprecedented.

When Comrade Dalvi went to Dahanu, fifteen to twenty thousand *Adivasis* had gathered at Narpad on the seashore to fix the wages for farm work. They were determined that they would not do bonded labour and would have the wages fixed. Comrade Dalvi took *Adivasis* to the hill in Kosbad. (Today there is an agricultural college there.) He talked to a few representatives to settle the wage rates and then advised them to go home.

When thousands of *Adivasis*, with sticks in their hands, went in an orderly procession from Narpad to Kosbad, landlords could not believe their eyes. They were stunned; they were terrified. Landlords who were used to beating *Adivasis* broke out in a sweat at the sight of the sticks in the hands of thousands of *Adivasis*. But not a single *Adivasi* misused his stick. Solemnly, quietly, they left in disciplined lines. Some landlords confessed their feelings, "Such a big gathering, but nothing went wrong. We had feared the worst. These Communists are highly disciplined." *Adivasis* walked through the stronghold of the landlords who daily brutalised them, but not a single hair on a landlord's head was harmed. This incident is noteworthy and especially for those who were alleging that we incited people to violence.

Adivasis were eager to build a great united force. They had learnt from experience that the larger and firmer the unity, the greater its power. They used to estimate the size of a rally by denoting a place where every *Adivasi* coming to the rally dropped a small stone indicating his attendance. The bigger the pile of stones, the bigger was the rally. When I went to Dahanu, *Adivasis* showed me many such heaps of stones giving evidence of big rallies.

As pressing a button sets a massive machine working, so *Adivasi* resistance started with the support of the red flag. The landlords' challenge was crushed. We had not expected such enthusiasm and unity from *Adivasis*. The centuries-old tradition of bonded labour was destroyed by *Adivasis*' great unity, hard resolve, and courage to risk all in the fight. The attacks and the daily beatings stopped. *Adivasis* were so assertive that no one dared raise a hand any more. This was the first victory won by *Adivasis*.

VII

Marriage Servants, Free Yourselves

When I went to the tribal region, there was a system of 'marriage servants'. In reality, these were debtors who worked as servants to pay off the debts. The ones who had taken loans for marriage expenses were called marriage servants. This practice had been in existence since old times. The *Thane Gazetteer* (Part I, pp. 155-156) describes the practice as follows:

> *Under the Marathas many of these tribes had been the bondsmen of the Pandarpeshas or high caste villagers. The name of bondage ceased with the introduction of British rule. But with many of the more settled of the wilder tribes, the reality of slavery remained and nominal freedom only served to bring them under new and harder masters. Formerly their masters used to pay their marriage expenses. Now they had themselves to find the funds. And as none of them had the necessary 40 or 50 rupees, most of them had to pledge their labour for a term of years. This term of years through Sowkar's carelessness and the lender's craft often developed into lifelong and sometimes into hereditary servitude.*

The system of marriage servants in this area would make one's hair stand on it's end. They were the moneylender's slaves in reality. The only difference was that they were not bought and sold by owners as in the system of slavery. Some *Adivasis* had told me, "My Seth took money from another Seth and sent me to work for him as his marriage servant." But such cases were quite rare.

The expense of a traditional *Adivasi* marriage was 100-200 rupees. When one wanted to get married, the first question was where to find this money. Since they did all the work without payment, they hardly had a few paisa's saved, leave alone such a big sum. Marriage was a natural and social necessity and it has even greater importance in *Adivasi* society. An unmarried person was looked down upon in his community. So marriage was necessary. But the decision to get married entailed a whole series of troubles because of lack of money. *Adivasis* were forced to borrow the money from the landlord or the moneylender. An agreement was signed at the time of borrowing whereby the borrower and his wife would do any work the lender demanded until the loan was fully repaid. Landlords and moneylenders maintained accounts in such a way that the loan was never repaid even if the *Adivasis* worked for years or even their whole lives. The borrower's descendants were forced to take over the loan through a promissory note. In this manner, generations of families were reduced to the condition of slaves.

The interest on these loans was exorbitant. I have seen a 100 rupees loaned at the interest of an *anna* for a rupee. That meant an interest rate of 75 rupees per cent per annum. Warlis were ignorant and illiterate and accepted the landlords' accounts and calculations. City people wondered why the loan could not be repaid if the couple worked steadily for a certain number of years. They reasoned that when the man and his wife worked day and night for the landlord, their salaries over a certain number of years would be enough to wipe out the debt. The answer was very simple. The wage paid to the marriage servants was zero. The man got a *dhoti* and *kurta*, at most a turban, and the wife got a *sari* (not quite nine yards) and a blouse once a year. Some landlords gave tobacco for *bidis*. But they never paid wages. That is why the loan could never be repaid. On the contrary, *Adivasis* considered it the landlord's kindness that he lent the money when they needed it and worked day and night, grateful for the rice, salt, and, on rare occasions, dal that they were given.

As it was impossible to repay the loan in these conditions, marriage servants worked as slaves all their lives. Generations worked for the landlord. Immediately on marriage, the couple had to go the landlord's house. They had to live where he told them to and do whatever work he told them to. Some landlords had the couple live together while others sent the husband to the house in the city while the wife worked in the fields. Once the wife was separated from her husband and kept on the field, the landlord could use her sexually as he pleased. The landlord would treat her as his property. When they were separated in this manner, all the couple could do was to weep. When I heard these stories, I remembered the incidents in the novel Slavery Revealed. I had to remind myself that what I was hearing were not incidents from a novel but reality. I told myself that I had to change this reality; that is the oath I and my husband had sworn.

The marriage servant couple did all kinds of work. They got up in the morning before everyone else and slept after the landlord went to bed at night. Throughout the day, they swept the house and the courtyard, washed the dishes, did the laundry, drew water from the well, made preparations for cooking, cleaned the stables and milked the cows, pounded and ground food grains, cleaned up after meals, looked after lamps and torches, cleaned the horse cart, lit the bulbs, fed and groomed the horse, gave the landlord a massage, carried loads over tens of miles, ran miles after the landlord's horse or horse cart, cleaned the toilets—these and thousands of other such services the marriage servants performed without payment to make the landlord's life pleasant.

I would ask them, "How could you bear to see your wives being dishonoured? Why didn't you run away?" They answered, "Where would we go? They would hunt us down and beat us and bring us back." They were right. Their world was limited. They had hardly any money. If they ran away and tried to work for someone else and if that person realised they were runaways, he would hand them over to the lender. If they were in a nearby village, the landlord would send his supervisors or musclemen to find them. They would beat the couple and drag them back to the landlord. And then the landlord would lock them up and beat them some more. It was not only the marriage servant who was beaten. Landlords would also beat his parents and brothers saying, "Why did you son run away? Give me my money." Where would they complain against the assaulters? There was no hope of justice from the courts. Simmington has written in his report:

> *If the debtor is slow or recalcitrant in making payments or rendering services, he is threatened, assaulted or beaten by Sowkar's agents who are often Pathans and Bhayyas. A man refusing to give his work for which he has taken a loan is sometimes improperly prosecuted and I regret to say that the Magistrates have sometimes taken a strangely perverted view of such prosecutions.*

Marriage servants worked like automata in the midst of the landlords' opulence. They seemed stupid. As they walked with their heads lowered, one wondered if they were deaf and dumb and blind. But the moment they had the support of the red flag, hundreds of *Adivasis* kicked off the shackles of landlords' and moneylenders' oppression and rid themselves of the sickening life of slavery.

Experience had taught marriage servants that they could not free themselves working individually. *Adivasis* planned and carried out the action for the liberation of marriage servants by themselves, without any outside help. The Kisan Sabha does not have any credit for it. *Adivasis* saw the red flag movement as a movement for their liberation. Liberation of marriage servants was a part of that movement, and so they planned and implemented it. They organised rallies attended by thousands and decided to free marriage servants. *Adivasis* at the rally were divided into four groups and each marched to landlords' houses. There they shouted the slogan, "Pick up your rags and pots and free yourself." The reference was to the marriage servant's belongings, which amounted to a piece of cloth or a handkerchief and an earthen pot. The call was to take what little one had and walk away from the life of slavery. The call brought marriage servants and their wives out of their masters' houses and they joined the protesters.

The groups marched through the villages for three days. In those three days, hundreds of marriage servants were freed. What they could not do alone, they had done united. All they had for support was the red flag. When the *Adivasi* groups went around with the red flag in their hands, landlords who had considered it their birth right to own marriage servants and their wives, sat silent behind closed doors and windows. *Adivasis* freed their brethren languishing in slavery without harming a hair on a landlord's head.

When I addressed rallies in Dahanu after the liberation of marriage servants, I could see that it was a new ray of hope that they had broken the shackles of years of slavery. The happiness on their faces was indescribable. They vied with each other to narrate how they were freed, what happened, how they defeated the landlords. A woman called Navashi came forward and said "We escaped that hell." I spoke to the women for a long time and they told me horrifying incidents of the hellish life they had escaped.

One point must be made here. Could one not marry without money? *Adivasis* found an appropriate solution to this problem. If there is no money, they do not perform the marriage rituals. For a small expense, the groom observes the tradition of giving bangles and a *sari* to the bride, which is called *korad*. The bride then goes to the groom's house and lives there.

For all practical purposes, they live as husband and wife. If the wife becomes pregnant, they perform an interim ritual as quickly as possible. Women are very eager and nag to have this ritual performed. Once it is done, a child born before the actual marriage has the status of children born after the marriage. There is an interesting recent incident. In 1967, a Warli named Rupaji Ozarya of Vadoli village earned some money enabling marriage and held his son's and his own marriage at the same time.

When they began to receive wages and other payments after the resistance, many Warlis organised their children's and their own marriages at the same time. Until then, they had lived as husband and wife according to the ritual described above, but had not been able to marry according to custom because they did not have money.

Two things happened after we left. Marriage servants were freed and started getting wages, which enabled some of them to get married. In the Warli community, it is the groom who pays dowry. If the bride does not want to live with her husband, she can get a divorce, but she has to return the dowry to the husband. If a woman decides to marry another man, that man has to repay the first husband. The village elders decide the matter after deliberation. They have to be given food and liquor. If a woman does not get along with her husband, or he beats her, or she loves someone else, she is free to leave her husband. If the first husband is not repaid the dowry, it can lead to fights. The village elders decide the matter. But a woman does not stay with her husband if she does not like him for any reason.

There was one more solution to the problem of lack of money. If a man is engaged to a woman but has no money to pay dowry, he lives with the wife's family. The girl's father and a couple of others go to his home and escort him to their home. An agreement is signed in the presence of village elders that the husband would stay with the in-laws for three to five years and live and work like a family member. After this, it is deemed that the dowry has been paid and the two are married.

VIII

The Call of the Red Flag

In October, around Dassehra, at Palghar, Dahanu, Bhoisar, Umbargaon, and Bhillad stations, you can see groups of Warlis carrying pots and pans, a box, sheets, leaves, and sticks; the men covered with sweat, wearing a loincloth, hair in a topknot; the women with just enough clothes to cover themselves, hair uncombed; and their half-naked children. The whole station has an acrid stench.

Why do these people assemble on the station? Landlords take them to various villages in the jungle to cut grass. In this region, the three to four months after Dassehra are hectic. The main work is harvesting the paddy, threshing it, and cutting grass. If these tasks are not done in time, it leads to a loss of thousands of rupees.

Grass is big business. After Saphala station on both sides of the railway tracks, green grass stretches as far as the eye can see. Some grass grows naturally while other is specially grown. To the east of the railway line, a lot of grass grows in the jungle, in rocky and hilly stretches, and on uncultivated land. This grass is well cared for and grown. Thousands of acres are exclusively grass lands, called Grass Mora. The land owners sell the grass to middlemen. Owners have earned profits of thousands of rupees and amassed wealth in crores.

It takes thousands of labourers to cut the grass at the right time. Because the period of cutting grass and harvesting paddy coincides, farmers are reluctant to put aside the harvesting work in their own fields and go to work cutting the grass. To make sure they would come to work at the specified time, they have to be paid money in advance. This practice of advance payments to engage labourers is known as 'tying a person' or contracting a person.

Landlords gave the task of engaging labourers to the middlemen, who in turn appointed supervisors to do it. The *Adivasis*' small stock of grains is depleted by the time of the festival of Holi. This is the time when the supervisors go into the villages. They tempt the needy with promises of paying anything from 10 to 25 rupees, and sometimes pay a part of the amount immediately, to 'tie the person' for grass cutting. The advance is later adjusted against wages. When the grass cutting is to begin, the supervisors gather all the workers engaged in this way. If someone tries to avoid it, he is abused, beaten, and dragged out of his hut. The Warlis are herded from their village to the nearest railway station and packed off on trains like cattle. The middlemen get 8 *annas* for every bale of grass for doing little. The supervisor makes 50-60 rupees per month during the season.

The landlords want the grass cut within a certain time frame. If the grass dries in the sun, its weight decreases and quality drops. It does not fetch a good price. If the grass is cut wet with rain or dew, it turns black and quality drops. Again, it cannot command a good price. That is why the grass must be cut at the right time. That is why the middlemen and the supervisors hustle to engage as many labourers as possible to cut the grass. Hundreds of workers are bound by advance payments. Some farmers do not take advances, but accept the work and take wages.

In this season, hundreds of workers enter the grass lands. Rows of workers bent over cutting grass with sickles can be seen from the railway train after Saphala. The labourers live in the grass lands until the grass cutting is done. During the cold nights, they light fires and sleep around them. If it rains, their condition is miserable. When they are at work cutting grass, the owner's supervisors watch them club in hand. They constantly shout to keep working to make sure nobody slacks off. Under the hot sun, the workers' bodies are pouring with sweat. But even when they are thirsty, they cannot go for a drink of water. They cannot take a break to smoke a *bidi*. It could bring down the supervisors club on their backs at any moment. Sometimes, even when nobody has done anything wrong, the supervisor would deliver a blow to one worker to terrorise all the *Adivasis*.

Adivasis' work was not limited to cutting grass. They had to make bundles of the cut grass, and then make five hundred to one thousand bundles into bales of about 500 pounds in weight.

Experience had taught them to do this work quite well. Grass made into bales is better protected from the sun and the rain. *Adivasis* did all the jobs from making the bales, pressing the grass and tying it into bundles, carrying the bales to the warehouses or the railway station, and loading them in the freight train cars.

Until 1945, the *Adivasi* farmer's payment for all this work was an *anna* or two. Or a bowl of toddy worth 2 *annas*!

During the Second World War, grass got a good price. The land owners made profits of crores of rupees. But the wages for grass cutting did not increase beyond 2 to 4 *annas*. Grass cutting was done through bonded labour. When I saw the beggarly, starving workers on the railway station, I thought of the crores of rupees that the owners had earned. Thoughts raged through my mind and I saw the truth that selfishness destroys humanity.

Kisan Sabha decided to get the grass cutting wages raised. In consultation with *Adivasis*, it was decided that the wages for a 500 pound bale of grass (that is, cutting 500 pounds of grass) should be 2.50 rupees. Considering the grass land owners' profitability, this amount was quite low. The owner's costs had been taken into consideration in arriving at this wage rate. The calculation included the expenses on cleaning the grass, guarding it, wages for grass cutting, transportation, pressing the grass, loading the freight cars, warehousing, and discounts.

After allowing for these costs, the land owners' profit was 11-12 rupees on every 500-pound bale. Our calculations were correct. This is confirmed by an interview of that time with the then revenue minister Morarji Desai: "By now, 40 lakh pounds of grass worth more than 1.50 lakh rupees must have been burnt." This gives the price of a 500-pound bale as 18 rupees and 12 *annas*. By paying an *anna* or two to the workers, the landlords made huge profits. We made the reasonable demand of a wage rate per 500-pound bale of 2.50 rupees in the jungle and 3 rupees in the port. The landlords rejected it. The winds of resistance started to blow.

The never-before success of the movements to abolish bonded labour and free marriage servants had given *Adivasis* confidence in the power of unity to solve the problem of fair wages. They went on strike for better wages for grass cutting. Not a single Warli went to work. The strike was completely successful.

In the initial stages of the strike, landlords did all they could to break it. For the flimsiest of reasons, *Adivasis* were locked up in jail and criminal cases filed against them. But this harassment embittered and angered *Adivasis* and steeled their resolve.

Land owners asked the government to intervene, using their usual propaganda weapon that Communists encourage violence. The strike was completely peaceful. Their plea was rejected. Then they made an appeal to the district collector that the government should not interfere in the matter. Years later, landlords told me—"to tell you the truth" in their words—that they had asked permission to get a lot of musclemen to soundly thrash the *Adivasis*. But their appeal was again rejected. Then the landlords devised a diabolical plan to induce the government to intervene with guns and oppressive measures and teach Warlis a lesson.

Landlords' Conspiracy

There had been many red flag rallies at Talwada village. Taking advantage of this fact, landlords spread a rumour on October 10, 1945, "Madam has called a public meeting in Talwada. But the landlords' musclemen are going there to disrupt the meeting and Madam's life is in danger. The red flag asks all *Adivasis* to go to Madam's rescue with sticks, sickles, axes, and anything that can be used as a weapon." This false message was relayed through passing trucks, shopkeepers, landlords' houses, and many other channels.

The plan worked. The gullible *Adivasis* believed the lie. *Adivasis* who hesitated to go out at night were scolded by their wives, "Madam's life is in danger. Why are you not going?" They said a prayer and went out into the night with whatever weapon came to hand. One old *Adivasi* from Upalat said, "When we heard that Madam's life was in danger, people even got up halfway through their meals and walked out with sticks in their hands." This was a cruel plan to exploit *Adivasis*' loyalty to the red flag and to me. At midnight about ten thousand *Adivasis* gathered at Talwada with sticks, sickles, axes, and whatever weapon they found. Many had come from 30 to 40 miles away. The police superintendent told us after a few days that thousands of *Adivasis* were coming from all directions. By morning about 30,000 *Adivasis* had gathered.

The landlords spread a rumour among *Adivasis* on the one hand. On the other, they informed the police that on the incitement of the red flag *Adivasis* had gathered in large numbers prepared to attack. They created panic and asked for police intervention.

The police superintendent arrived there with a huge contingent. Without making any inquiry and taking the landlords' word as the truth and obeying the landlords' wishes, the police started firing from the tops of police vans on the *Adivasis* quietly waiting for the rally to begin. From the night of October 10 to about 11 am on October 11, police vans patrolled the Mumbai-Ahmedabad Road near Talwada, firing on innocent *Adivasis*. Five *Adivasis* were killed in the firing. Hundreds, including children, took bullets. The exact number of wounded was never known.

Warlis reasoned that, as they had not done anything wrong, the police had to be firing on the red flag. So they sat there thinking that they were protecting the red flag. The thought of the courageous Warlis standing foursquare in the face of bullets to defend the red flag thrills my heart, bows my head in respect. The blood spilt at this spot reminds us of the *Adivasi* martyrs of red flag.

When no one had arrived by afternoon to address the rally, *Adivasis* began to wonder. One of them went to our Khattalwada office to make enquiries. Comrade Ranadive had just reached the office. He was stunned to hear about the police firing. He could not believe it. He went to Talwada immediately. He explained the facts and asked *Adivasis* to go home. Even as he talked to the Warlis, bullets continued to be fired and Comrade Jethya Gangad fell to one of those bullets.

For 15 hours, *Adivasis* stood firm in the face of firing. If Comrade Ranadive had not reached there, *Adivasis* would have continued to sit there who knows how long. What the firing could not achieve, a single word from the red flag did. Warlis operated on the simple idea that they had gone there on the order of the red flag and would not leave without an order from the red flag. They left carrying a fire within that landlords had killed five of their brethren and had deceived them.

The government issued its standard format statement justifying repression, saying that hundreds of farmers had engaged in stone-throwing. The Adivasi Seva Mandal, which was a Congress party organisation and now has the blessings of the government, issued a statement that was published in the *Bombay Chronicle* on October 25, 1945.

> *Whether the firing was justified or whether it was excessive, we were not able to ascertain. It is, however, clear that the police were firing from the roof of the van, which was converted into a sort of armoured car. No one from the police seems to have been hit though there was stone throwing. The firing, we fear, must have been indiscriminate. We feel that there should be an open and independent inquiry into it.*

The government did not institute an inquiry. There was a departmental inquiry that concluded that the firing was justified, reported the daily *Chitra*.

After the firing, oppression began to grind the region. The police banned carrying sticks and assembly of more than five people. Comrade Dalvi, three or four workers, and 125 *Adivasis* were arrested.

News of the firing reached Comrade Parulekar and I on the morning of October 11 when Comrade Kama Ranadive came to our Kalyan residence to tell us about it.

On October 9, the Thane district collector had invited me to discuss the Warli strike and some other matters. Until then, the situation had seemed 'normal' to the government.

The announcement of the rally was an utter lie. We had not scheduled a rally. I was not well and was at Kalyan. Our workers were in the villages meeting *Adivasis* eligible to vote in the coming elections and helping them write applications to get their names entered on the electoral rolls. We were astonished at the news. Until we learnt of the landlords' plan, we remained uncomprehending. We felt baffled.

On October 11, 1945 the then milk commissioner of Mumbai. MD Bhat, wrote to Comrade Parulekar saying, "The situation in Umbargaon and Dahanu talukas is having a serious adverse effect on the supply of grass to Mumbai. I would like to talk to the two of you." The grass cutting strike had affected the supply of grass and therefore of milk.

On October 12, we met MD Bhat and told him about the oppression and about the possibility of our arrest. He said, "We will see about arrest. But leave immediately and work towards a compromise. It is essential that an agreement is reached and grass cutting begins." We understood the underlying message and started on the evening of October 13. The milk supply to Bombay was difficult enough that the Gujarat Mail made an unscheduled stop at Sanjan station to enable us to reach the area quickly. At Sanjan, we had our first taste of oppression. On the orders of the police, no *tonga* would take us. But when it became known that the train had stopped at Sanjan especially for us, we finally got a *tonga*.

The Thane district collector came to Sanjan after the police firing. We met him at Homi Daviyarwala's bungalow in Sanjan on October 14. We told him what we knew about how and why the landlords had announced the meeting. The landlords demanded that the collector banish us from the area.

The collector wanted negotiations and an end to the strike. He invited for discussion Daviyarwala, Devdekar, and Pethe on behalf of the landlords and Comrade Parulekar and I on behalf of the farmers. The landlords responded, "We do not recognise the Kisan Sabha. We will not talk to these two as their representatives." District collector Bedekar said calmly, "You talk to me. They will also speak to me." We presented our calculations before the collector and put forward the demand of 2.50 to 3 rupees. We explained why that demand was justified, supporting the argument with numbers. The landlords said they would not pay anything more than 1.50 rupees. There was no compromise and the talks failed.

When the talks failed, oppression began again. On October 15, Comrade Parulekar, I, and some comrades were banished from the area.

Before we left, we told *Adivasis*, "Maintain your unity. Do not be afraid. Do not cut grass unless you receive 2.50 to 3 rupees." The person who took this message came back to tell us about the great enthusiasm and resolve of the *Adivasis*. Their resolve was such that they watched any middle class person walking by on the suspicious that he was there to break their unity. They were so fierce that no collaborator dared go into the jungle.

The order banishing us from that area was illegal, and police superintendent Sharif Khan had to revoke it on October 25.

The landlords' plan succeeded to the extent that they were able to spread the false message about the rally, induce *Adivasis* to arm themselves and assemble, get the police to fire on them, banish us from the area, and oppress *Adivasis* with the help of the police. But their aims were not achieved. The strike did not break. The landlords' mighty blows proved ineffective and boomeranged on them.

In the period of our absence, landlords committed inhuman atrocities against *Adivasis*. They would give the police the names of people who were inconvenient to them. The police would arrest them. This was described in a statement by the Adivasi Seva Mandal, published in the *Bombay Chronicle* of October 25-26. It says:

> *We had complaints that the landlords, whose names were mentioned to us, made lists of tenants whom they found inconvenient and handed them over to the police, for getting them arrested. We found that after the firing the people from the nearby villages were so panic-stricken that they had left their hamlets and hid themselves in the jungles. 10 or 12 days they had to go without food. People were afraid to disclose their injuries and give their own version. They feared that the police would arrest anyone who came forward and their fear was not groundless.*

During the days of oppression, landlords' houses were the homes and refuge of police officials and personnel.

A Parsi landlord called Barjor had a house in Ghanori village. Officer Salvi and other policemen stayed there. Jehangir Patel, Sukanchand Marwadi, and the police chief of Ghanori brought *Adivasis* from surrounding villages to the house for questioning on the pretext that they had illegal guns, but in reality for beatings. They beat up many Warlis on the pretext of possession of illegal guns. One Warli called Nanhu Gharat was beaten to death. On October 22, he was called to Barjor's house. He was hit with sticks on his legs as he was being taken there. Then they hit him on the limbs and the torso with stones wrapped in thick cloth. The cloth was wrapped so that the stones would not leave marks on the body. He was punched on his ears. After the beating, he was made to stand bent over and his loincloth was taken off. They poured kerosene on his buttocks and tried to set it on fire with a burning stick.

Nanhu started screaming in pain. He lost consciousness and fell to the ground. He was beaten again as he fell. All this happened in the presence of the police officer and his men. When Nanhu was conscious, he cried out in agony,"Sir, my home has never had a gun for generations. Even if you kill me, how can I produce a gun?" Nanhu was kept there all night without food or water. According to Nanhu, Barjor Seth told the police chief, "He hasn't been beaten enough. If you shove a stick up his arse, he will produce not one but two guns." Nanhu could not walk the next day. The police took him back to his hut. They had pity on him and were saying among themselves, "How will these people ever wash off such sins."

Ladkya Tambda was beaten by the Seths in the presence of the police, punched in the chest, whipped with a horsewhip, and swung by his topknot. Hirya Ramaji was beaten to a pulp. Pasrya Rama was beaten because he attended the rally on Saturday. Vanshya Jinya had attended the rally at Osarwira but could not report what was said there, and so was beaten.

Kanha Tanhya Gharat was being beaten when his wife tried to stop them and she was also beaten. Ladkya Holya was starved for two days and beaten saying "You, the king of the jungle! You, a red flag follower!" Ladkya Navshya Morgha was beaten with the landlords' belt. While beating him, the landlord said, 'I am the saheb today. Don't call me Seth. I have government orders to beat you'. Chetya Handwa, a 70-year-old man, was beaten because he did not stop his children attending the red flag rallies.

Devaji Rupaji Pathera had a 20-year-old daughter called Laxmi. The police told her to give up the gun belonging to her father. When she said "I do not know whether he has a gun or not," the police caught her by the neck. They lifted her up and slammed her down again and again.

They threatened to rape her. When she started to scream, they let her go. Thami from Amboli village was grabbed, her *sari* was pulled, and she was threatened with rape. They threatened to stab her private parts with the bayonets of their rifles. All this because she was helping her father to evade arrest.

Landlords, moneylenders, and the police unleashed a reign of terror from October 15 to 25. Many *Adivasis* ran away into the jungle for fear of torture.

Landlords had thought that the extreme brutality and oppression would terrorise *Adivasis* and they would capitulate and report for grass cutting work. They thought, "We will bring them to their senses. They will go back to work within two days."

But the *Adivasis* who had woken up from centuries of slumber frustrated their plans. *Adivasi* unity and resolve remained steadfast. They did not lose courage. Not a blade of grass was cut in the jungle.

Adivasis would find some way to meet me in Mumbai and tell me the heart-wrenching stories of their trials and tribulations. The newspapers in Mumbai helped expose these atrocities. The *Free Press Journal* editor Natarajan and *The Sentinel* editor Horniman gave invaluable support. Their reporting shaped public opinion that put pressure on the government.

The shortage of grass in Mumbai threatened a calamity. As the days went by, landlords started to worry that the grass would dry out, prices would fall, and they would make losses of thousands of rupees. *Adivasis* refused to cut grass until the orders of banishing us from the area were revoked and the people in jail were released. The landlords could not hold out. Their dream of cowing down *Adivasis* died.

The situation compelled the government to think. The orders of banishment were revoked and the people in jails were released.

The *Adivasis* had won. Their joy knew no bounds. To prevent losses, landlords competed to recruit workers. Kisan Sabha had demanded a wage rate of 2.50-3 rupees. The landlords now gave 3.50-4.50 to prevent losses where they had earlier refused to pay anything more than 1.50 rupees. They did not have to worry about whether they could afford the rates. It was the landlords who surrendered, not the *Adivasis*.

We Party workers were proud to be a part of this victory. My mind, which had numbed from hearing about the inhuman atrocities, now started to find joy. Comrade Parulekar had tears in his eyes.

Adivasis once again experienced the power of organised class struggle and unity. They were not intoxicated with this victory, but reflected seriously and marched ahead. The people who truly deserve credit for this success are the *Adivasi* followers of the red flag.

IX

The Next Step

The Adivasi Seva Mandal's report of 1945-46 talks of the courage of the *Adivasis*: *"They have reached a state of mind that will no longer tolerate abusive treatment at the hands of landlords and moneylenders. They have understood that their strength lies in unity."*

To outline the next steps of the *Adivasi* movement, Kisan Sabha held a rally on January 21, 1946 in Mahalakshmi village. The rally was for farmers in Umbargaon and Dahanu talukas. But *Adivasis* from Palghar and Jawhar talukas came to see what the red flag rally was all about. Some *Adivasis* had walked as much as 50 miles to attend this rally. Around 15,000 *Adivasis* attended. They exulted at the victory they had won over the brutal might of the landlords. In this rally, for the first time they donated thousands of rupees to the Communist Party fund. This they have been doing for years since then. When we were banished from the area, an *Adivasi* had brought to the Party office the 900 rupees that Comrade Dev had left with him.

At this rally and convention, two important resolutions were passed.

Landlords maintained the accounts, recorded the share *Adivasis* paid, and showed dues from *Adivasis* for years. Dues from previous years, extra share as a penalty for those dues, and the regular yearly share—all these, correct or false, added up to thousands of kilograms of rice as due from *Adivasis*. Landlords used threats to extract as much paddy as they could. No receipt was ever given. The farmer only got the burden of dues. *Adivasis* starved themselves to grow the crop only to give it to the landlord, and still the dues did not decrease. *Adivasis* wondered how this could happen and suspected that landlords cheated them. But they did not know what could be done.

Landlords not only took a share of the paddy crop, but also pulses, vegetables, eggs and poultry, and fruits. If *Adivasis* did not give up these, share of paddy was increased. This had gone on for years, and the farmers' outstanding dues had grown to crippling amounts. An important resolution was passed at the Mahalakshmi convention on this question. The resolution was that the unjust and unpayable dues must be declared void. The resolution was expressed in the slogans: "Do not pay additional dues imposed in the last three years." "Do not pay any old dues."

The second resolution passed was that all payment be made in the form of paddy and no vegetables, pulses, fruits, and other such should be given.

The farmers immediately implemented both the resolutions. All the unjust outstanding dues vanished. What individual farmers had not been able to do for years was made possible because all together boldly and publicly announced their intention to do it. Landlords had been extracting unjust dues and so their position had no support in law or ethics. They had no moral courage and gave in without protest.

Adivasis were vigilant and saw to it that these resolutions were implemented everywhere in the tribal area. If they found a landlord or his men taking away any produce other than rice, they stopped them. Some landlords and their supervisors tried to take away other produce on the sly, but they were stopped, questioned, and made to return the produce. Some *Adivasis*, in an excess of enthusiasm, made the landlord bow before the red flag. Landlords did not have justice on their side and *Adivasi* enthusiasm was great. That made it easy to win these demands.

The *Adivasis* from Palghar and Javhar who had attended the Mahalakshmi rally joined the struggle. They also got the demands that the Dahanu and Umbargaon farmers got. They abolished bonded labour. They abolished the *bhudas* or farm serf system. They voided illegal outstanding dues and enforced payment of dues only in the form of paddy. At the request of Palghar taluka farmers, I addressed a farmers' rally in Palghar in May 1946.

On their own initiative, *Adivasis* had expanded their movement from Umbargaon to Dahanu and from Dahanu to Palghar and Javhar. We were there only to give them support. From January to October 1946, we built the Kisan Sabha and the Party organisations on scientific principles. Comrade Parulekar made an invaluable contribution to this task. For long he had conducted study sessions for *Adivasis* and explained ideas in simple language. But he always had one condition, that I should begin the lecture. I moved daily among *Adivasis* and had a close relationship with them. I would discuss a typical incident in their lives, and Comrade Parulekar would use that opening to move to a discussion of ideas. On the one hand, we were preparing the farmers politically and intellectually and on the other, we were trying to resolve their economic and social problems through the Kisan Sabha. Our office was like a beehive in those days. Every day hordes of farmers came to our office from villages near and far. They would complete their court business, and stay overnight, and return satisfied and proud to their villages the following morning.

After Dassehra and Diwali, jungle clearing starts in a big way in addition to cutting grass and harvesting the paddy crop. Like most other work, wages for jungle clearing were very low at four to 8 *annas* and in some places just 1 to 2 *annas*. The jungle clearing had also been done by bonded labourers. Kisan Sabha decided to demand fair wages for jungle clearing.

Another demand was that the wage rate agreed for grass cutting in 1945 must be paid in 1946. There was no doubt whether the rates were affordable to the landlords. They had paid more than the agreed rates in 1945. But the political situation had changed in 1946.

The previous government had been dismissed and the Congress Party had come to power. The founder of Adivasi Seva Mandal, BG Kher, had become the chief minister of Bombay Province. Morarji Desai was the home minister. The collector of Thane,

Bedekar, was transferred and replaced by Almola, who had suppressed the historic Bardoli Satyagraha. This stooge of imperialism was transformed when the Congress party came to power and turned into a staunch Congress loyalist.

The *Adivasi* region is mountainous and covered in jungles. There is excellent teak and other wood used in building construction. The trees in the jungle are divided into sections called *koop*. The government, through the forest department, auctions the sections to the highest bidder. Traders purchase rights to the sections and employ hundreds of workers. *Adivasis* felled the teak and other trees, cleaned and chopped them, loaded them on bullock carts or trucks, sorted them according to quality, and finally cleaned the land in the section to hand it back to the government. To fell a tree, they first tied a rope near the top of the tree. Then they began to chop the trunk of the tree. When the tree was ready to fall, they pulled on the rope to bring it down where they wanted. Some workers entered into an arrangement to cut a hundred trees of a certain thickness to earn a certain wage. The wages earned are quite low under this arrangement because supervisors count trees without regard to thickness. Others worked for daily wages.

In 1946, the firewood and building wood business was good. Traders made crores in profits. But the workers earned 4 *annas* a day whether they worked on per tree or per day basis. The Simmington report comments on this: *Daily wages are 4 annas and when 6 or more workers who have worked together divide the payment amongst themselves, each has not more than 3 annas or even less.*

Once the tree cutting begins, contractors build a pandal nearby. The supervisors or contractors stay in these pandals until the work is done. In those days, the pandal was the centre of oppression and abuse. The supervisors tried to cut *Adivasis*' meagre wages and pocket the deductions. Workers doing the heavy labour of axing trees were not allowed a break for a smoke or a drink of water. Great discontent smouldered in *Adivasi* hearts over these matters.

Kisan Sabha had demanded a wage rate of 1.25 rupees a day. Taking into consideration the contractors' profits and the *Adivasis*' hard work, this was a reasonable demand.

For cutting grass, the 1945 wage rates of 2.50 rupees in the jungle and 3 rupees in the port were demanded. We thought that, since this demand had been accepted in 1945, there would not be any dispute over it.

In July 1946, the district collector Almola called a meeting of the representative of the grass land owners and Kisan Sabha to discuss and fix the wage rates. When Comrade Parulekar and I went there, we were told that the meeting has been postponed. But the reality was that the meeting had been abandoned following the government policy of not granting any form of recognition to the Kisan Sabha.

Kisan Sabha demanded daily wages of 1.25 rupees. Considering the hard work, the rising prices of consumer goods, and the wages paid for similar work elsewhere, the demand was lower than reasonable. The amount was not enough to support even a low standard of living for a family.

The contractors who earned crores of profits were not willing to pay 1.25 rupees as daily wages. The local magistrate tried to find a middle path and announced a wage rate of 1 rupee per day. This had the effect of providing indirect support to the forest contractors' rejection of the rate of 1.25 rupees.

The market price of grass in 1946 was higher than in 1945. The grass land owners had paid higher wages than Kisan Sabha's demand in 1945. Wandrekar had said in his statement that the Kisan Sabha's demand was reasonable. But with the aim of weakening the Kisan Sabha, Almola declared the rate of 1.50-2 rupees for a 500-pound bale of grass. The land owners who had been paying higher rates stopped paying them.

Adivasis were determined not to work for lower wages. Struggle over this issue began again. Kisan Sabha decided to call a strike until both the demands were met.

Adivasi unity was so strong that, within 48 hours of the announcement of the strike, forest clearing activity stopped for miles around. I was amazed at their organised and rapid action. This strike was extraordinary. As turning off a main switch would instantly put off all the lights in a building, so the decision in

Dahanu right away stopped jungle clearing in an area of hundreds of miles.

Adivasis had a novel method of passing messages. They tied toddy leaves to a stick and also attached a note about the decision to strike. This stick was taken from village to village. When the stick arrived at a village, jungle clearing work stopped there. The unity and loyalty of Warlis made the strike successful in a short time. Grass cutting came to a standstill. *Adivasis* also stopped driving the hundreds of bullock carts needed to transport the produce.

As the strike succeeded, the government started making its moves. The collector issued an order directing officers in the taluka to organise public meetings to ask people to work at the wage rate declared by the government.

On October 22, 1946, the civil service officer called a public meeting. People boycotted it. No one attended a single public meeting called by government servants or officers. The government servants got tired of this and gave up on public meetings.

Adivasis had, on their own initiative, stopped driving bullock carts. The traders, contractors, and landlords told *Adivasis* to drive the carts because the Kisan Sabha had not asked them to stop that work. *Adivasis* answered using the idea of a permit, which they knew from using permits at the ration shop. They told the traders and contractors to get a permit from the Kisan Sabha to use the bullock carts at fair rates, only then would they drive the carts.

One day some work took me to our office in Dahanu. Comrade Kama Ranadive was sitting cross-legged on the floor and writing something using a small trunk for a table. As she finished writing a sheet of paper, she gave it to the landowners who sat there grim faced. I had no idea why they were there.

After the land owners left, Comrade Kama explained that even for the land owners who agreed to pay the Kisan Sabha rates, Warlis would not start grass cutting work or drive carts without a permit from the red flag. That is why the landlords were at the party office to get permits from the red flag. We issued a directive to work for those landlords who would not or could not suffer financial losses and those who were ready to pay the Kisan Sabha rates.

The *Adivasi* struggle was progressing peacefully. Landlords and moneylenders were planning to repeat the strategy of 1945. They started filing criminal cases against farmers.

A rumour was spread that Kisan Sabha was going to observe October 10, 1946 as martyr's day and organise a rally at Talwada. The police superintendent and the collector rushed to the spot with 150 armed police personnel. The collector had meant to help the landlords. But the landlords' plan was foiled. *Adivasis* did not fall into the trap. Nobody went to Talwada.

The government and the landlords were eager to impose Penal Code 144 and unleash repression. They filed false cases of housebreaking and theft and arrested 55 *Adivasis* from Raytali and nearby villages and took them to Dahanu jail. *Adivasis* felt that they had to rescue their innocent brethren arrested without reason.

Thousands of *Adivasis* set off for the Dahanu jail. When Comrade Kama Ranadive heard of this, she intercepted the *Adivasis* on the way to prevent trouble. She persuaded them to go back. They went back reluctantly and only out of respect for the red flag. When many such tricks failed, landlords and their goons began direct attacks on *Adivasis.* One *Adivasi* farmer was so brutally beaten near Vangaon village that he died in hospital four days later. Even after this, *Adivasis* did not fall into the enemy's trap. They remained serious about their aims and true to their path.

Days went by. The strike could not be broken and the grass was lying uncut. Some landlords agreed to pay the wages we had announced and to withdraw the false cases against the *Adivasis. Adivasis* were not satisfied with this. They demanded that, as a penalty for filing false cases, landlords should pay the villages a sum decided by the village as compensation. Some grass land owners acceded to this demand. They reasoned that if the grass were not cut, the losses would mount to thousands of rupees; better pay a few hundred rupees to get work done. Gradually most landlords accepted the grass cutting wage rate demanded by the Kisan Sabha. No one paid attention to the rate declared by the collector. The landlord Jugalkishore and some other millionaires decided that, whatever the losses, they would not accept the Kisan Sabha rates and would use the government's repressive force to compel *Adivasis* to cut the grass. The repression did happen, but the grass was not cut.

Adivasis have a generations old custom that when someone commits a crime, the five village elders deliberate the matter and the person found guilty pays a fine to the village. *Adivasis* had followed this custom when they asked grass land owners to pay penalties. Some paid it. To the *Adivasis*, this was nothing new. But the government knew nothing of *Adivasi* culture and started the propaganda that the Communists are running a parallel government. We did not understand anything of this at first. On making enquiries, we learnt about the penalties. We did not know whether to laugh at the government's policies or to weep over them.

The jungle clearing strike was going on peacefully. Traders had about 2.5 crore rupees invested in this business. There were no signs of the strike ending. Pessimism spread among the traders. They grew restless at the thought of losses of thousands of rupees. When the atmosphere seemed conducive to a compromise, the welfare officer for the province AH Khan held talks with the Timber Merchants' Association president Babubhai Ponda and his associates and Kisan Sabha's Comrade Parulekar and I. The rates were fixed such that, whether payment was per day or per trees cut, workers would get 1.25 rupees daily.

Other demands were accepted, for example, compensation for injury or loss of a limb. An agreement stating these demands was drafted. In the presence of Khan in his bungalow, Comrade Parulekar and I signed the agreement on behalf of Kisan Sabha and Ponda of Dahanu and another person signed on behalf of the traders. The Ponda High School principal Karnik signed as the independent witness.

Thanks to the mediation of the province officer, this issue was resolved in a manner acceptable to both sides. The Timber Merchants' Association approved the agreement in its general body meeting. I went into the jungle to explain the terms of the agreement to the *Adivasis* and ask them to go to work.

No one imagined that the Congress government would reject an agreement acceptable to both the parties and signed in the presence of the province officer.

Congress rulers had other plans. The Congress ministry ignored the agreement between the jungle contractors and the Kisan Sabha mediated by the province officer. To destroy the Kisan Sabha and the Communist Party, the government declared a state of emergency in Thane district on November 14, 1946. About 200 *Adivasis* were arrested. Many others were placed under house arrest. All workers of the Kisan Sabha were banished from Thane district.

I was in the jungle holding meetings to explain the details of the agreement to the *Adivasis*. There were no newspapers in the jungle. I learnt about the declaration of emergency only when I finished explaining the agreement to the *Adivasis* and returned to Khattalwad. The unexpected frenzy of repression numbed my mind. Comrade Parulekar and I returned to Kalyan. On November 21, 1946, we were issued notices of expulsion. We left Thane district.

Adivasis continued the strike in the face of repression. government repression reached the point of sending in the army. *Adivasis* resisted the repression with incomparable courage. *Adivasis* won in the final analysis. But they paid a cruel price.

From November 21, 1946 to January 14, 1953, Comrade Parulekar and I could not openly set foot in Thane district. We had been expelled from 1946 to 1948, were underground from 1948 to 1951, were in prison from 1951 to 1953, and finally returned in February 1953. Thousands of *Adivasis* came to welcome us at the rally in Mahalakshmi village. I was overcome by emotion at their loyalty, love and fervour. I wondered whether I deserved this loyalty, whether I could bring any benefit to these hard working people. Comrade Parulekar often went silent from strong emotion and that happened now. After a while he said, "We are so small compared to this sea of humanity! What tremendous loyalty, zeal, capacity for resistance! They have broken the shackles of slavery with their own strength. We were merely instruments."

X

State Repression and Adivasi Resistance

In the 20 years of struggle in Thane district, *Adivasis* had to face state repression on three occasions. Each assault was more severe than the previous one.

In 1945, the government attacked for the first time. The next onslaught was in 1946-47. In 1956 during the united Maharashtra movement, the third attack happened. It wrings my heart to think of the torments *Adivasis* suffered in the resistance to these attacks.

The repressive measures of 1946-47 had the single aim of demolishing the power of the Communists. With the support of the Communists, *Adivasis* won demand after demand and so long as this continued, their loyalty to the Communist Party could not be weakened.

This is why the government disregarded the agreement reached between the grass land owners and the *Adivasis* and started oppressive actions. That this interpretation of government actions is correct is confirmed by Morarji Desai's interview, a report of which was published in the *Free Press Journal* on January 22, 1947.

> *He [Morarji Desai] was not aware of any understanding that may have been arrived at between the Timber Merchants' Association and the Kisan Sabha at the instance of Prant Officer, who wittingly or unwittingly, may have been a party to that agreement. He is now on leave and has been transferred. The government could not bind itself to any and every act of the Prant Officer done on his initiative.*

The government's refusal to recognise an agreement made by the province officer was a strange example of administrative procedure. It was a lesson to us. Once they decided to destroy the movement and the Party, those in power were willing use any means to achieve that goal and would justify those means. The province officer Khan was amply rewarded for having brought about a compromise. He was asked to go on leave and then transferred.

When the Timber Merchants' Association realised that the government was willing to use its coercive power to crush the struggle and support them, one of their representatives went even further than Morarji Desai. He made an about-turn and went so far as to say that they had never signed any agreement with the Kisan Sabha. Their statements were ridiculous and lacked credibility. The *Free Press Journal* report on the matter in the January 29, 1947 issue is worth reading:

> *'The President of the Timber Merchants' Association attended talks. In the recent matter of the government, Warlis, and Communists, whoever the President talked to, he had refused to meet any Communist leaders. Not only that, he had agreed to a wage rate of 1 rupee per day. He denied that he had accepted the main clause of the agreement of 1.25 rupees wages per day. They might as well have said that Ponda was never the President of the Timber Merchants' Association, that there never was any special officer, that there are no Communists and no Warlis, the whole thing is just a figment of someone's imagination.'*

Comrade Parulekar wrote many appeals and memoranda to the cabinet of ministers from November 19 to December 5, 1946. On December 17, a compromise was reached. There was no change in conditions from December 10 to 21. Why then did the government resort to oppressive actions? It seemed possible that, in the absence of accurate information, the government had misunderstood the situation and therefore adopted the wrong course of action.

On this assumption, we presented detailed statements about the ground realities to the government. But in fact it was us who had misunderstood, not the government, because of the illusions about the national government and party policies.

Government Begins Repression

The memoranda presented by Comrade Parulekar had no effect. The government had taken deliberate steps to demolish the *Adivasi* movement and *Adivasis*' loyalty to the Communist Party. On January 20, 1947, Morarji Desai held a press conference. His statements offer substantial proof of the government's intentions. One such statement appeared in *The Times of India* on January 21, 1947: "I am not interested in any settlement brought about by the Communists. Anything which helps Communists in their nefarious activities will not be tolerated."

The report in *The National Herald* of January 22, 1947 is even more explicit: *"Shri Desai also made it plain that the government would not countenance any compromise which would give full control over the Warlis to the Communists." Once the government began repressive action with the resolve to destroy the Communist Party, it only grew worse. The government went so far as to bring in the military to crush Adivasi resistance.*

News of our expulsion and the arrest of Warli activists spread like wildfire. *Adivasis* began to stop work on their own initiative. Grass cutting stopped. Farmers on jungle clearing work began to shoulder their axes and leave. Bullock cart drivers abandoned the carts carrying grass and wood where they stood and walked away. Even without a leader or party worker, the work in the jungle rapidly but peacefully came to a standstill.

The government and the landlords had calculated that, once the leaders were expelled and the backward people given a few incentives, they would surrender, meekly accept an assault on their organisation, and return to work. This was comprehensively disproved. *Adivasis*' response was unexpected to the government and the landlords. Their scheme of weakening the Communists' hold failed. They did not know that, after the struggle of 1945, it was a new *Adivasi* they faced. They were frustrated in their aims.

During the initial stage, Kisan Sabha had compromised and offered to cooperate. But the government had rejected the gesture and now had only two choices. One was to adopt a fair and unbiased policy and accept the agreement already reached. The other was to use force to cow down the people. The government and landlords chose the second path.

To break the strike, forest contractors would threaten timid *Adivasis* and ask them to report for work. These people would go to work, but before leaving, they told their clansmen, "They abuse us and threaten to beat us. What can we do? Please help us." The next day, hundreds of Warlis would go to the place of work roaring red flag slogans. Those at work would be waiting for an excuse. They would immediately stop work and join the crowd. Barring a few exceptions, all the jungle clearing work stopped. The forest contractors began to devise plans to start the work again.

Frivolous cases began to be filed against *Adivasis.* Cases were filed against about 400 *Adivasis* and many were thrown into lock-ups. To teach the *Adivasis* a lesson and to keep them rotting in jail, district collector Almola started interfering in judicial matters and started using his discretionary powers to crush the resistance. With that objective in mind, he passed three special orders:

1. The cases of crimes, atrocities, and violence against *Adivasis* would be heard every day. The idea was to deny *Adivasis* the time to prepare their defence. In such a one-sided trial, the prosecution would find it an easy decision to send them to prison. This order effectively gave the lower courts the power to sentence the accused without worrying about the question of justice.
2. Bail for Warlis would be set at large amounts of money. The objective was that poor Warlis would not be able to get bail and would rot in jail before any crime was proved in court.
3. Warlis would not get bail unless they gave the undertaking that they would not attend any rallies and would not participate in any activities of the Communist Party. This third order makes it clear that the main aim was to terrorise Warlis to stop them from participating in Communist Party activities.

The number of cases filed against *Adivasis* was so large that a separate court was established with a special magistrate. This court only heard cases related to the red flag. This court came to be known as the red flag court.

Government, Landlord, and Moneylender Alliance

During this period, we received valuable support from renowned legal professionals—lawyers T. Godiwala, Nimachwala, and Shah from Mumbai and Prabhakar Hegde from Thane, and barristers Rajani Patel and Sushila Patel from Mumbai.

Nimachwala lived in Dahanu in 1946-47 and fought the poor Warlis' cases. *Adivasis* drew great comfort from the fact that a lawyer of the red flag was always in Dahanu to help them. The district magistrate tried to take away this legal support by abusing his power.

A false case was filed against Godiwala that he addressed public meetings. He used to go into Dahanu for legal work. Using the excuse of public speeches, he was expelled from the area. That same night he was attacked. He was on his way to Dahanu station to return to Mumbai. As he got off the *tonga* at Dahanu station, landlords' goons attacked him and beat him on the head and legs with sticks. The hat on his head was crushed, but it saved him. Almola used to think he ruled Thane district and no one could call him to account for his actions.

Nimachwala needed to visit the Warlis in lock-up to gather information regarding the cases. Personnel at even the lower levels of police hierarchy began to place obstacles in his path. Not satisfied with this, Almola finally expelled Nimachwala, too, on December 11, 1946.

The expulsion of Godiwala and Nimachwala was a violation of their right to practice their professions and was blatantly illegal. Nimachwala and Godiwala wrote letters of protest to home minister Morarji Desai. They wrote to the Bar Association in Mumbai to bring the incident to their attention. There was an outcry in the newspapers. Almola had to rescind the expulsion orders. Nimachwala went back to Dahanu and stayed there tirelessly working day and night on the Warlis' cases.

Landlords and the government combined forces to completely demolish the Warli hamlet of Musalpada near Dahanu station. Some Irani landlords had gone to Musalpada to threaten Warlis and get them to go to work and there had been a row. The landlords went away. They returned at three in the afternoon with about 10 policemen and 50 goons. The village was razed to the ground. The men were not at home. The goons and policemen entered the huts and threw out the utensils; they broke the earthen utensils, crushed the aluminium ones, and broke the stone grinders. With rifle butts and axes they demolished the huts. If a home had honey collected from the forest, they spilt it on the ground. If somebody had paddy, they scattered it. Bullock carts were smashed, their wheels broken into pieces. The old people and children who were at home were beaten and their cloths torn.

Before they left, they took away the money they found—poor people's savings stashed on the lofts or in baskets—and goats, chicken, and eggs. After that, government servants and moneylenders' goons went into the village every day and warned: "If you don't end the strike and don't give up the red flag, the consequences will be serious. We will bring the military and kill you all."

After this incident, *Adivasis* came to Mumbai to meet me and explain the situation there. I personally took the *Adivasis* to newspaper offices so that the atrocities would be made public and then curbed. *Adivasis* told their story in their own words. When newspapers took up the issue, the government—whether to placate *Adivasis* or mock them, government alone knows—gave the generous sum of 5 rupees as compensation for every hut destroyed and considered its duty done.

Landlords and moneylenders, with the connivance of the government, harassed *Adivasis* in an attempt to make them surrender. But Warlis had lost their fear of jail. They did not waver. After years, they had an opportunity to display courage and took a kind of pleasure in it. They accepted the challenge.

Adivasis avenged the mayhem in Musalpada. One either side of Dahanu station, Irani landlords have big orchards. *Adivasis* had been forced to work as bonded labour to grow flowers and fruits. They did much other work, too. *Adivasis* had already been seething with resentment and then the Musalpada incident happened. Hundreds of *Adivasis* had their revenge and destroyed the landlords' orchards, cut down every tree.

False Charges against Me

I was arrested on February 6, 1947 under Section 153 of the Indian Penal Code. A case had earlier been filed against me that I made speeches inciting people to violence. I had been expelled from Thane district. I was summoned to the court for the hearing of the case and went to Thane district to attend court. As I came out of the court, I was arrested for violating the expulsion order. To issue a summons to attend court and then to arrest me for entering the district in violation of the expulsion was wrong and laughable. But the intention was to arrest me under any pretext. I had to spend only two or three hours in the dirty lock-up in Thane. Barrister Rajani Patel made immediate arrangements for my release.

The propaganda that I made speeches to incite people to violence had been going on for many months. Landlords, moneylenders, and Adivasi Seva Mandal functionaries made arbitrary statements about it. No case had been filed because all the allegations were false. At all my speeches, government shorthand stenographers and the police used to be present. If I had really made speeches supporting violence, the government would have lost no time in arresting me. Even responsible Congress workers talked nonsense about my speeches. SR Bhise, secretary of the Adivasi Seva Mandal, said in a statement to a Marathi newspaper dated December 25, 1946: "Queen *Godutai* Parulekar made a speech in October at a rally in the Dahanu forest. In that speech, she asked Warlis to maintain peace as follows: 'The moneylenders are drunk on power. We will dig a big pit and bury them all in it. We will plant a tree there and raise our red flag on the tree'."

If I had really made such speeches, the government eager to arrest me, would not have let me remain free for even a moment. Even a little effort to find out the truth would have shown Bhise his mistake. But he was so prejudiced that he did not stop to verify the truth of the statement. The reality was different. In my speeches, I used to speak critically about the moneylenders' regime. Earlier, Congress workers used to parrot, "We will not retain the institution of moneylending. We have to finish that system." The comment in my speech was that the red flag had started digging a pit and the moneylending system would be buried in it [not the moneylenders]. There was nothing illegal or encouraging of violence in it. But my opponents did not have the level-headedness or the prudence to see that.

The case against me did not go on for long. The witnesses called by the government to prove that I made speeches promoting violence gave testimony to the effect that I told Warlis, "Remain peaceful and continue the struggle peacefully. But always remain united." One of the government witnesses said, "Madam asked people to be peaceful." Angered by this, the prosecutor demanded, "What did she ask them to do to be peaceful?" He replied, "Madam said, don't start fights or riots. No disturbance . . . and all that." When all the testimonies had been heard, there was not even enough evidence to file charges and the case was withdrawn. My opponents were dejected.

The opponents' plan was two-pronged. One, expel Godiwala and Nimachwala to take away the legal defence of the Warlis. Two, arrest me under a false charge and tell the *Adivasis*, "The woman is in jail. Who will you go to now?" They thought this would bring *Adivasis* to their knees. But their plans failed. They were maddened with rage. With the government's help, they unleashed a reign of terror.

Adivasis had two options. One was to surrender and accept defeat and the other was to resist. They chose the second. On one side was the combined might of the government, landlords, moneylenders, and their thugs. On the other side was the unity of thousands of *Adivasis*. These two powers faced each other on the battleground.

Rampaging Repression

The government expelled all the leaders and workers of the Kisan Sabha from the district. Hundreds of *Adivasi* workers were thrown into jails. The police force deployed was a 100 strong at first, then 500, and finally 1,000. A network of police stations was spread through 139 villages. The police patrolled day and night and went around yelling at people. Additional motorcars and messenger vans had been deployed. To demolish Communist Party propaganda and to effectively convey the government propaganda, the police superintendent had requisitioned many more propaganda vans.

The police officers and their men stayed on the landlords' estates. The landlords treated the police to royal hospitality. They hired thugs to act as guides for the policemen and to provide them with information. They gave the police the names of *Adivasis*, named the inconvenient *Adivasis* who were to be arrested, and identified individual *Adivasis*. With these preparations, they started their attacks on *Adivasis*.

In the village of Kosbad, a Marwari landlord and the police beat up the women. Their men had run away into the jungle. The women were threatened, "Call them back. If they don't return, we will rape you."

In Gholwad, *Adivasis* were beaten on landlord Dasharath Seth's property. A policeman pushed Navsha Warli to the ground and started to beat him. Another policeman pulled at his topknot. Other policemen hit him in the ribs. The officer hit him on his ears. Some Warlis were hung upside down and beaten. Some were kept hungry for two days. Some were whipped on their backs until it bled. All this was done because they would not reveal the names of those active in Party work. Warlis bore the beatings and the tortures but did not reveal any names.

Special officer Save went to Nikana, Vadhana and other villages to pacify *Adivasis*. But people did not go to hear him speak, which angered him. He started making wild statements. I was told that he once said, "I am going to tell the police to open fire if they see more than three Warlis in one place." To save a Warli's life was no better than a dog's or a cat's life! Warlis reported all this to us. Later, we also heard that the district collector was present at the rally in Kasar village. When no male Warli attended that rally, he was furious. He told the police to beat up the family members of the Warlis who were hiding in the jungles. The idea was to make the Warlis come out of the jungles and arrest them.

Repressive actions began to rampage through Palghar. The police killed two children of around 10 years because their father could not be found. One Warli's body was twisted. Two militant activists Comrade Navsha Varatha and Comrade Zhatebaba spent months underground in the Navaranavari hills. When they were found, they were beaten until their calves bled. Comrade Devadi Tandel's mother was told that the police had orders to kill her son and bring his dead body if he did not present himself before the police. Comrade Tanhu Walvi's house was burnt. He lived in the jungle with his elder son. His wife took the younger son to another village. One of the children went missing. The family was broken up. Many families were destroyed in this way during the struggle.

When the police found an *Adivasi* at home, on threat of arrest, they would demand meals, food rations, chicken, and eggs. Chandra Devaji and Chandrya Mahadya were threatened with jail and made to give 20 rupees each. We received many such complaints with details including names. There were terrible beatings. Even then, *Adivasis* who used to be scared of the sight of one policeman now stood ready to resist thousands of policemen running amok.

The belief that the combined force of the government, landlords, and moneylenders would defeat *Adivasis* within a week was proved wrong. *Adivasis* built their organisation throughout the region and girded themselves for battle.

Adivasi Resistance

When hundreds of *Adivasis* were thrown into prison, others ran away into the jungle and hills to escape arrest. Many party workers as well as many farmers went underground. Underground comrades began to direct the movement from the jungle. Repressive tactics became harsher in an effort to capture those who were underground. *Adivasis* put their experience and ingenuity to work to prepare their defence. They observed that the police never went around the jungle in ones and twos but always in small groups. They learned from this and they too never went around singly but moved in groups. To overcome the police, they formed groups or units of 100, 200 or even 500. They would tell me, "Madam, police parties go around. So we formed our own parties. Ours are bigger than the police parties." The groups or units were highly disciplined. One young man from every family joined a unit and he brought food rations to last him a certain number of days. After working for those many days, he would go back to his house and another young man would take his place. These units began to patrol the jungle day and night. Each unit had a leader. He decided where the unit would stop for rest or to eat. On his orders would the unit march again. It was strictly forbidden to light a *bidi* at night without his permission. This was a precaution so that the light of the *bidi* would not give them away to the police. There were other people who had the task of gathering information on the movements of the police and the landlords and moneylenders as well as of carrying messages about these movements throughout the area. There were some people appointed to regularly bring us information. That was their only task. People watched the doings of the government and the landlords and took action at the right time.

Adivasi resistance reduced the atrocities by the government and landlords. But *Adivasis* could not bear in silence the brutal treatment of their brethren. They decided to counter-attack.

Barjor, a Parsi landlord, had poured kerosene on the Warli Nanhu Gharat and tried to burn him alive. Warlis took revenge. *Adivasis* saw Barjor and Chandu Talathi travelling in a lorry near Pimpalshet village. They were suspicious of their movements. Some 3,000 *Adivasis* surrounded the lorry and destroyed it. They taught the landlord a lesson but did not kill him and instead let him go. Due to the *Adivasis*' aggressive stance, the police, landlords, and their thugs started losing the courage to attack.

Adivasis moving around in large units to defend themselves made the police and landlords wary. To break the *Adivasis*' collective movement of awareness and resistance, police resorted to firing in Nanivali village in Palghar taluka on July 1, 1947. When information came that 2,000 *Adivasis* were going to Nanivali, a police sub-inspector went there with a police contingent. The police ordered the *Adivasis* to disperse, but they would not move. The police opened fire. Five innocent Warlis died. Many took bullets and were injured. Dr Kulkarni extracted a bullet from one *Adivasi's* shoulder in the Communist Party main office. But *Adivasis* did not lose courage. Those who met me said, "Madam, in this struggle, we won't surrender even if it kills us. So many have died; so many have suffered so much. How can we give up now?" I used to be astonished at their resolve. But I could not do anything, and that was suffocating.

Around that time, there was another firing at Kosbad. I heard it from the people who came to meet me. They described the firing. "Madam, the firing happened near the hill at Kosbad. Comrade Govind Andhere has served in the military, and he told us to lie on the ground. We lay down and escaped injuries. But chips were blown off the sides of the hill." What can I write about this incident considering that the government claims that the firing never happened?

Nanivali firing led to wanton loss of Warli lives. We demanded an open inquiry into the firing, but the government refused. In October 1945 when there was firing, BG Kher had demanded an open inquiry saying: "Human life is sacred and when death takes place by firing, the government must feel it their duty that an open and impartial inquiry should be held into the causes and justifications of that firing."

BG Kher had proclaimed the sanctity of human life and demanded an open inquiry into a firing in 1945, but he forgot his own arguments in 1947. He had become a defender of the bureaucracy that killed five innocent *Adivasis* in broad daylight. The demand for an open inquiry into the firing was dismissed. As the repressive actions grew harsher, *Adivasi* resistance became stronger. As the resistance became stronger, the repression grew harsher. Finally, the government went so far as to bring in the army to break Warli resolve.

Guerrilla Tactics in the Jungles

Hundreds of *Adivasis* were locked up in the prisons at Yerawada, Thane, Nasik, and Visapur. The prisons were full. Sentences ranged from six months to seven years. Many *Adivasis* went underground, for seven months, nine months, a year. When their demands were accepted, many voluntarily gave themselves up. Some were never caught; they never surrendered. *Adivasis*, while underground, capably performed the task of giving courage to and guiding the entire community. They lived in the hills and jungles and devised an appropriate response to whatever situation they faced. An *Adivasi* once lived a month in a hollow he made in the thick boundary wall of a field because he could work better from there.

The police committed atrocities, but they became afraid of moving alone in the jungle. Even armed police did not have the expected success when facing *Adivasis* who knew every path in the jungle and the hills. *Adivasis* took part in large rallies and processions almost every day and afterwards disappeared into the jungles and hills. They stopped the movements of the police. They blocked roads in narrow mountain passes with boulders and logs of wood. They placed obstructions on other roads, too. It became difficult for the police to move around in the jungle. The roads used by forest contractors' vehicles were dug up and rendered unusable. Deep in the jungle is a village called Sukadamba. Five armed policemen had gone there. Thousands of *Adivasis* stopped them in the gorge at Sukadamba. The police dropped their guns and ran away. *Adivasis* took charge of the weapons. We told them to put the guns back where they had been.

Adivasis were cruelly beaten and ill-treated in many ways. Women were sexually assaulted and humiliated. Landlords and moneylenders had always abused them and now the police added to it. This infuriated the entire *Adivasi* community, filled them with a wild energy. What might they not do in extreme anger, we wondered. It became difficult to hold them back, to calm them down. The entire community had joined the struggle. *Adivasis* did not eat at home. They carried food rations with them. After some days, their women placed *bhakaris* at an agreed place and the men would pick them up from there. The police were now stretched. On hearing that 200 *Adivasis* were arriving at Tumbh village, a hundred policemen went there, but found nobody there and had to return empty-handed. In a similar incident, they made a futile trip to the gorge near Jalawai village. This kind of news appeared often in the newspapers. *Adivasis* would start a rumour and watch the police go on a wild goose chase. They were no longer afraid of the police.

One day hundreds of *Adivasis* went to Gholwad station. Some Warlis were being held in a grass warehouse there. They were freed and taken away amid loud slogans of victory.

During those days, once 11 *Adivasis* were arrested and held in the lock-up near the district magistrate's court in Palghar. When this news came, thousands of Warlis went to Palghar and surrounded the court. They demanded the release of the 11 *Adivasis*. They later told me that, on seeing such a large number, the district magistrate and other employees trembled in fear. The magistrate immediately released five *Adivasis* and promised to release the other six the next day. On this promise, the *Adivasis* left. But the magistrate moved the six overnight to Thane jail. A few *Adivasis* came to see us in Bombay. They were disturbed that their six brothers had been moved to Thane jail and the district magistrate had deceived them. They wanted us to approve their plan. Their plan was that thousands of *Adivasis* would march to Thane jail and free the six. Their logic was simple. If hundreds had marched to Palghar jail and freed five, thousands would march to Thane jail and free six. It took us a day to explain why their plan was wrong and to dissuade them from acting on it. Comrade Parulekar explained the matter from many angles and then sent them back.

Nobody knew when and how *Adivasis* would gather at a place. In the jungles and crevices, *Adivasis* had organised in such a way that hundreds of people would come from all directions at just a whistle. They behaved in such an ordinary manner that no one would suspect that anything unusual was going on. They carried out all work smoothly. Some would overtly speak against the red flag but have entirely different plans in mind. Their language, gestures, and whistles proved very useful. Nobody ever worked out how, when all was quiet and there was no movement, hundreds of people assembled all of a sudden.

For years, landlords had used *Adivasi* women to satisfy their sexual urges. This happened on their farm estates, which were the centres of atrocities. *Adivasis* had burned in anger. To make it worse, the police stayed in those same premises when they brutalised *Adivasis* during the struggle. *Adivasis* decided to destroy these symbols of oppression, the landlords' houses in the jungle.

Remnants of broken walls could be seen in some places for many days afterwards. In other places, nothing was left of the estates. No civilised person should be surprised that, once *Adivasis* found their strength, they would destroy the places where their women had been dishonoured. When the citizens of France destroyed the French prison Bastille, history forgave them. They were praised as having marched on heaven. History will judge it forgivable that Warlis destroyed the seats of cruel oppression in their own and their women's defence.

Efficient Underground Organisation

Hundreds of *Adivasis* were in prison. To demoralise them, nobody was allowed to meet them. But such tactics do not work when an entire community joins a movement. The letters *Adivasis* wrote to their brethren in prison to keep up their courage give testimony to their perseverance, resolve, and unity. The farm work of the *Adivasis* in prison did not suffer. Other *Adivasis* in the village tilled their fields. The following letters give an idea of the kind of letters free *Adivasis* wrote to those in prison.

> *To Laxman Barkya and other Warlis from Rankol, namaste from their families. We are all well. Tell Viththal Barkya, we have harvested your crop. Your family members are fine. Do not worry. The village is looking after your wife and children. We have not lost courage. You, too, do not lose courage. Do not weaken even if you have to stay in jail for a few more days. Our lawyer of the red flag is working for you. So do not worry and be at ease in the jail. The crops of all the people from Rankol and Shelta have been harvested. So do not worry at all.*
>
> *Yours*
> *Maya Devaji Vayada*
> *Lahangya Navshya Varatha*
> *Harji Bajya Sutar*
> *Rishya Shidawa Labad*

> *To Daji Majhya Salkar, Rajya Vithya Bhomar, and other people from Raytal, regards from their families. Do not worry about us. We have made arrangements for your crop. We have harvested everyone's crops and stored the produce. Even if you have to stay in*

jail for a few more days, it is okay. All the people of Raytal are firmly united. All are helping us. That is why we have no problem. You, too, be healthy and happy. We have courage. You, too, do not lose courage. Do not worry about what happens here. The lawyer of the red flag is working to get you bail. Be well. Lal salaam.

Yours
Kondya Devaji Varatha
Madya Tanhya Shelkar
Vithal Janya Varatha
Ratna Davi's mother
Pateri Raja

The *Adivasis*' underground organisation was efficient as well as skilled. They managed to get letters into the prison through all the security. They managed to meet Comrade Parulekar and I though the police watched all railway stations and villages. They led our workers into the jungles without anyone finding out. During this period, I spent 15 days walking through this territory to guide and encourage party members and safely returned home.

As the struggle progressed, *Adivasis* announced their demands again and again through various means. They distributed the following demands from Charoti village.

1. Pay 1.25 rupees per day for cutting trees.
2. Fix the charges for the bullock carts that carry the grass and wood.
3. Release the *Adivasis* who have been arrested.
4. Cancel the orders expelling the leaders from the area.

Sheets bearing these demands were tacked on the trees along major road where landlords, moneylenders, forest contractors, and government officials passed and also where they lived, and along the main roads. The opposition was nonplussed on seeing this. government officials and servants wondered how these people could come through heavy security, accomplish what they have come to do, and get away with no one the wiser.

Along with this announcement, they put up another letter for the police. This letter said that policemen came from farming families and so should not brutalise fellow farmers, fire on them, and shed their blood. All these notices went up in the jungle in one night. The next day, police officers could only watch helplessly. Some police had seen the poverty stricken and pitiful state of *Adivasis* and wondered at the conditions. They were secretly pleased at *Adivasis* scoring points. Senior officials noticed this. Rumours say that seven policemen were suspended. More officers were brought in for supervision. The police superintendent commented on the unbreakable unity of *Adivasis* in an interview, "Warlis have divided themselves into small groups. Their organisation has deep roots in the district and stands on a firm foundation. They have their own couriers. They get all the information."

The Army Arrives—and Goes Back

Communist Party members in villages led the struggle at risk to their own lives. Most remained steadfast to the end. They named others to take over leadership responsibilities if they were arrested or had to go underground. Even hundreds of police personnel proved ineffective against such a strong organisation and the government decided to call in the army.

A regiment of the Maratha Light Infantry stood ready at Kalyan. The advance guard of the regiment entered Dahanu. This unit had to be sent back. Then the government appointed MM Moore Gilbert, infamous for repressive action against the Satara Patri government, as additional district police superintendent. But he, too, had to be sent back soon due to public pressure.

When *Adivasis* learnt that the army regiment had arrived, not only were they not frightened but they decided to put all their might into a final battle. In these critical times, the entire civil society stood with the *Adivasis*. *Free Press Journal, The Sentinel, Bombay Chronicle, Navyug, Jai Hind*, and other newspapers raised their voices in support of the *Adivasi* cause. These newspapers were opposed to Communists in some matters and, on those matters, had written bitterly critical comments. They had campaigned against Communist workers. But even so, they declared that the demands of the people enslaved for generations were legitimate and their fight just, and that it was wrong to bring in the army against them. NM Joshi, Datto Waman Potdar, Prof. Wadia, and other progressive leaders in Maharashtra publicly spoke in support of the *Adivasis* and criticised the decision to deploy the army. The Maharashtra Congress Committee had made certain recommendations at the time which show that the demands of the *Adivasis* were just.

Narhari Parekh, a follower of Mahatma Gandhi and volunteer of Sarvodaya movement, wrote an article on the struggle in Harijan and said that the *Adivasis*' demands were just. The pressure from important newspapers, independent-minded progressive leaders of Maharashtra, Sarvodaya movement workers, and the public forced the government to retreat. The military was sent back and so too was Moore Gilbert. On April 5, 1947, BG Kher made an announcement about freeing the jailed *Adivasis* and announced some concessions.

The Warlis released from prison received the welcome accorded to brave warriors. In Dhanori, villagers collected 45 rupees and threw a feast for their leaders. Some released *Adivasis* received so many invitations from other villages that they did not eat in their own homes for as long as a week.

While *Adivasis* admired them as brave leaders, Morarji Desai and the Congress ministry reviled them as thugs. Regarding these poor people as thugs was an indication of the elite's contemptuous attitude towards *Adivasis*, ignorance, absence of sympathy for the poor, and prejudice.

Adivasis were released from prison, but the orders of expulsion against us were not rescinded. The government hoped to win *Adivasis*' loyalty by releasing them and giving them a few concessions. But the government was disappointed. We returned in 1953. Until then, *Adivasis* were implementing the new concessions and carrying on the daily business of life. But our expulsion and arrest pricked their minds. The opponents were squawking through their newspapers, "*Adivasis* are fed up of the red flag. They have now come under the Congress banner." Neither the Warlis nor we ever paid any attention to it. They received a fitting reply in March 1953 when, after seven years of banishment, Comrade Parulekar and I held our first rally at Mahalakshmi. Hundreds of *Adivasis* gathered, raising the red flag and shouting its praises, rushing like thirsty creatures running towards water.

Achievement of the Struggle: Class-Conscious Farmer

The fire of the struggle that began in 1945 consumed the practices of land slavery, marriage servants, bonded labour, wood and grass cutting for a pittance of 1 and 2 *annas*, exorbitant crop shares and crippling amounts of unpaid dues, and other exploitative practices. On one side, *Adivasis* displayed tremendous courage; on the other side, government, landlords, and forest contractors unleashed extreme repression. The power maddened rich went to war with state power, armed police, money, and muscle power. They were defeated by the starving, half naked *Adivasis* on the strength of their willingness to stake all, their unity, and their unwavering faith in their goals. *Adivasis* won a dazzling victory. Out of this battle was born a class-conscious farmer.

Comrade Rupaji Kadu, Comrade Govind Andhere, Shidawa Sapata, Devaji Tandel, Navsha Varatha, Shirad Bhonar, Zhatebaba, Tanhu Walavi, Marya Ireem, Phelya Dhangada, Kakadya Sutar, Comrade Dhakat Sutar—I could not give all the names, there are so many! Hundreds of *Adivasis* lived in the hills and jungles, burned under the sun, and suffered torments. They would say, "Madam, what is this pain we have to suffer. We are in one place and our wives and children are somewhere else! We are lucky if we get *bhakari* and make do if we don't. Our legs swell from walking and climbing until they bleed. The police are looking for us and we are always on the run. If we are caught, don't ask how bad it is."

One thing always pained me that these people never expected any rewards. They never craved publicity or fame. Nobody ever garlanded them or published their photographs. They were never offered good jobs. But they wanted one thing, that Madam should meet them. They wanted Comrade Parulekar to know how bravely they had fought and how they never wavered in their resolve.

They would be very happy when Comrade Parulekar praised them saying "You are brave." They did not expect anything else, did not care for anything else. They knew that their struggle was to free themselves from the shackles of slavery. The struggle was their duty. Even today, they want only one thing. To improve the conditions of the poor and to eliminate poverty, power must be in the hands of the poor. They are willing to undergo any trials to make it happen.

The unparalleled struggle of the farmers of Dahanu, Umbargaon, and Palghar is a golden page in the history of the farmers' movement in Maharashtra. The legal concessions that were granted to the exploited farmers of Maharashtra after 1945 are owed to a large extent to the Warli farmers and their struggle. Minimum wages, increased farm wages, and reduction in shares of produce and many other legal concessions have been given to other farmers, too. However, in the absence of farmers' organisations, they have remained on paper in some places. If farmers' organisations rise to implement these concessions and if farmers unite to take the next step, *Adivasis* will have a sense of fulfilment that their struggle bore fruit.

XI

Underground Tour

After expelling us and arresting many other workers, moneylenders and landlords took advantage of our absence. Believing that victory was within their grasp, landlords, moneylenders, and their hangers-on would stand at Western Railway stations such as Dahanu, Palghar, and Umbargaon and jeer at *Adivasis*. With aggressive gestures, they would say, "Where is your red flag now? Where is your Madam? Our government has thrown her out. She is in jail. Where are your red soldiers (red flag workers)? Madam has gone; the red flag has gone. You have us to deal with now. Where will you go? Scream as much as you like, no one will come to your rescue. We will tie you to the trees, hang you upside down, and beat you. We will hitch you to the plough and make you work as bonded labour." Others would say, "Go, get lost! Go to Madam. Go to the red flag. They will give you food. They will give you wages. Why come to us now!" The state repression of *Adivasis* had intoxicated the landlords and moneylenders. At homes and on farms, wherever they saw *Adivasis*, they expressed their feelings in abusive talk and cruel laughter. *Adivasis* told me, "The landlord pranced on the railway station platform and mocked us." *Adivasis* ignored the taunts. They went about their work with expressionless faces. But they were boiling with rage within. They felt that I should go there once so that they could tell me about the landlords' doings, discuss what would happen next and what to do, see me once again among them, and speak their hearts out to me. Because they had not seen me for a long time, some of these disadvantaged people felt worried. They wondered what if Madam never came back. What would happen! They would send a message, "We will protect you with our lives. Just come to us once and give people courage." As I had spent many years in prison, I was not afraid of arrest. But people drew strength from my being free. I had to think of how it would affect the movement if I went to the area in contravention of the expulsion order and got arrested.

We discussed the situation and decided that I should go back there once. I said goodbye to all the party workers. Comrade Parulekar placed a reassuring hand on my back and said, "Go. Take care. But accept whatever happens." In working towards a good cause, one has to put aside one's feelings. Everyone knew that if I were arrested, I would receive the maximum sentence. If I had been imprisoned then, I would not have seen Comrade Parulekar for four years. We had been underground from 1947 to 1951. It might have happened that Comrade Parulekar would be underground and I in jail. But I was not arrested and that separation did not happen. Thanks to the *Adivasis*' love and loyalty and the bungling of the bureaucracy, I went around Dahanu and Umbargaon talukas on foot for 15 days and then returned safely to Mumbai.

"First Get Back My Husband!"

We left for Mahalakshmi in a car. People from Mumbai go to Mahalakshmi. The Goddess is believed to answer devotees' prayers. Nobody stopped us on the way. I got off at the turning before Charoti village in Dahanu taluka. The car continued on. It helped that I knew the area well. I confidently went to the house of the village policeman. The woman of the house came forward on seeing me and started talking loudly, "You have got my husband in jail. Get my husband back now!" I went cold at her words. I had gone to Charoti before the repressive action began, and the chief police officer had spoken bravely. I had said then, "You are the police chief of the village. Think carefully about it." He had replied with emotion, "I am not afraid. I don't care about anything." The policeman had stayed the night in the house where I was staying. We had spent the night talking. He was enjoying the newly acquired role of a leader. That is why he was taken to be a

Communist Party worker and was arrested. His courage waned as soon as the atrocities began. He and his wife were both afraid that he would be stripped of his post of Police Patil. Later he tendered an apology out of fear of prison and was released. When I went to his house, his wife had been arranging his release. I had no idea of any of it. At her demeanour, my face fell. I was disheartened. I began to suffer doubts. What was still to come!

The woman was not willing to listen to anything. She just kept saying, "Get back my husband." It was risky to stay there any longer. I left. I went to a hut in a hamlet nearby. I could go into any hut. Everybody in that village knew me, so I was spared or things would have been difficult. In this hut, two women were pounding paddy to separate rice. On seeing me, they got up and left immediately to call the men. But I told them that it would take time for the men to get there and that it was risky for me to stay there that long. They understood what was needed. One of them picked up my few things bundled in a dirty cloth and put the bundle on her head. She started for the house where I had asked her to take me. We walked through the forest, crossed the road, and reached Vadhana village on the other side.

There was energetic movement as soon as people saw me at a distance. Children jumped off embankments and raced to inform others of my arrival. Somebody cleaned the veranda of his home and spread a sheet. Nobody said anything but the change in the atmosphere and the surge of energy were palpable. My confidence was renewed. The boisterous activity of the children and the quiet happiness of the adults permeated the air. The house I went to was situated close to the main Dahanu-Kasa road. It was not safe to stay there for long. People quickly made me tea. We decided where to hold the meeting and I immediately sent people to inform the workers nearby. We started for the next destination walking by the hills for cover. People watched until we disappeared from sight. To make sure that nobody observing us should guess our meeting place, we zigzagged and reached the place at around eleven in the morning. The tea and the Warlis' pleasure in my being there rid me of physical and mental tiredness. The hills rose on both sides of our meeting place and a stream flowed close by. Some *Adivasis* were sitting there. Others stood guard. Within half an hour, some

25-30 *Adivasi* chiefs gathered. Some had brought tea and others had brought *patani bhakari*. The discussions went on for two hours. We discussed all that had happened. The *Adivasis* gained confidence and enthusiasm from seeing me there. I was happy that the discussions were satisfactory.

"Madam, Take Care . . ."

At around two in the afternoon, we moved to a different spot. It was a long walk. The shade of trees and a breeze protected us from the sun as we climbed the hill. The path was very narrow and sloping. On one side was the tall mountain and on the other a deep gorge. The path was so difficult that Warlis said they seldom took their cattle on that path. I used a stick for support and walked with slow steps. *Adivasis* walked in front of me and behind me carrying sticks, bows and arrows, and slings. Warlis often warned, "Madam, walk slowly." When necessary, they took me by hand.

It felt like evening in the jungle near the top of the mountain. I could not see any path. Where were they taking me through the vegetation? Just then we came into a clearing about 15 feet square. It was right near the top of the mountain. The Warlis quickly pitched sticks in the ground and covered them with leaves. It made a lovely pandal. Sheets were spread to sit on. Someone brought cold mountain water to drink. They took out the things they had brought and made tea. They also had *patani bhakaris*. As I was taking the tea and *bhakaris*, I learned that the clearing was used for hunting wild peacocks. The mountain top had more such places created specifically for hunting the peacock. The sun was going down. When it grew dark, Warlis built campfires just big enough to provide warmth and started chatting. I worried that the fires would be seen at a distance. They said, "Don't worry. The jungle is so dense that the fire will not be seen. Besides, the wood is smouldering and the flames are not big." We talked long into the night in the warmth of the fire. It was a good place to speak freely and without any anxiety. We discussed many things such as what a landlord says; who pays wages and who does not; who uses force; where are the police, how many are they, and what do they do; who joined the government and the landlords out of fear; how many new members have joined and who they are; who are underground, and where and how do they live; what do the people say; how are the families of the people in jail; what are the plans for the next action; what tactics should be adopted; what should be our policy in fighting repression.

Finally I fell asleep in the early hours of the morning. Since I did not have to get up early the next day, I slept until late. Since there was no milk, I had tea without milk and with jaggery. I wanted to see what kind of place it was and I started to walk. The clearing was surrounded by dense forest. As I made to enter the forest, the Warlis stopped me. They said, "Madam, if you go into the jungle, you will lose your way. You will be lost and walk around hungry and thirsty." They were right. You could not even see a way out of the clearing. I could not even tell from where I had entered the place. There was no path to see. For a person unfamiliar with the jungle, it would be not only difficult but impossible to find the place. Only Warlis knew the paths and places in the jungle.

That day I told the *Adivasis* that in spite of precautions, I could still be captured while getting to the north of Umbargaon taluka. I told them that even if I were caught, they must remain united and continue the struggle whatever the difficulties, and success would be theirs.

"The Red Flag Has Done Great Things"

In the evening, we climbed down the mountain on the other side and reached Avandani village. A small boy flew swift as a bird to the village to give the message of the meeting. Navsha had had a crib in his home. I slept in that house that night and got up early the next morning. People started teasing me, "Madam, a baby was born at night and you didn't wake up."

The Warlis had stayed up all night talking. I went in to see the mother and the newborn. On a mat was spread a thin cloth and the child lay on it. The mother had bathed in hot water and was lying near the fire. When I inquired about the diet, I was told that after delivery the woman would eat rice, rice soup, chicken if any, and, during the season, toddy. Three days after delivery, the woman would go to work in the fields or elsewhere. In that empty, desolate mud hut on a thin cloth lay the wealth of the nation. The sight shook me to the core of my being. I could not but compare this with the mother and child in an urban educated family.

It was late by the time we ate dinner. Warlis believe that women are dirtier than men. Women cannot cook for a guest. To show respect for a guest, men must prepare the food. Women could pound the paddy and grind the spices. After the meeting at Avandani, I started for the next village. We zigzagged on the way and it took a long time to get there. The path was such that it was impossible to move fast. We were walking through a jungle of bamboo and other trees. Mosquitoes bit us on the exposed parts of legs, arms, and face. The bites swelled and bled. If I drew my *sari* over my entire body, it would get caught in the thorns and make it difficult to take a step. I was at the end of my wits. It was hard to put one foot before the other. At such times, the Warlis would start talking about some amusing topic to help me through. Scratching the bites all over the body and wiping the blood, we finally reached our destination. But by then, the entire body was burning.

A Party worker, Comrade Pathara, was in jail. I met his mother in a field. She said, "I am not worried. The red flag has done great things. My son is a member. I have given my son to the red flag." She never asked me when her son would be back or when she would see him, but said with pride that her son was a member of the red flag. The old woman's words made my heart ache. I forgot all the difficulties, the tiredness, the mosquito bites, the torn clothes, and the burning body. My eyes were wet when I thought of Comrade Parulekar. I wanted to tell him what I saw and heard. But would I go back to Mumbai or would I be arrested. For long I reflected on the richness of experience in our lives.

The next stay at Bapgaon village did not go well. My host and his wife were afraid. Compared to the old woman in the field, these young people were cowards. They were waiting for me to leave the village. I was very angry at first and I spoke my mind. It had no effect on them. I was disappointed and became melancholy.

Such incidents made me wonder why I bothered to entangle myself in these matters. I could have lived a comfortable life in Mumbai. But then I thought that a large community would produce a few cowardly and selfish people. The sacrifice and idealism of the Warlis would bring me back to my senses and remind me of my responsibility.

In Bapgaon, I heard the phrase 'stitching a house'. I had heard of stitching clothes but never stitching a house. But they really stitch together leaves and lay the sheet on the roof of a house. All the rainwater flows to the ground and does not leak into the house. Because they do not have tiles, *Adivasis* protect themselves from the rains and the sun in this way.

There was a dance that night at Bapgaon. I heard the sounds of a musical instrument and came out to see the dance. The Warli dance is meant to be danced and not merely watched—it is for the dancers and not for spectators. It produces a kind of mesmeric state. Warlis can dance for four and five hours to the tune of the instrument and the bells on their sticks. Young men and women form a series of semi-circles and lose themselves in the dance. If anyone can take the purest pleasure in being alive, it is them, the Warlis.

I met some people in Bapgaon and then started for our next destination.

"Who Can Catch Me?"

It was dawn when we reached the next destination. It was a good meeting in that place. We had walked a long distance. I had not had a bath for days. It was winter and I did not feel like a cold bath when I was tired from walking. Finally at Sutrakar the next day, I had a bath at five clock in the morning in the light of a fire. There was great activity in that hut to make arrangements for my bath. They had brought the water at night. The men had built an enclosure. The women had been asking since one in the morning, "Should we heat the water? Is it time?"

Everyone knew that I was in the village. Even if they could not meet me, people were happy that I had been to their village. I would realise it at the moment of leaving a village. All the men, women, and children would find some reason to stand along the road to see me off. Sometimes they would stand on the mountains in a long line and follow me with their eyes until I disappeared from sight. At such times I felt that, with such support from the people, how could anybody catch me? How would they ever find me? I never stayed at one place longer than one day and one night. In those days anybody could enter an *Adivasis* hut at any time. They never had any conception of stopping people from entering their homes without permission nor felt any need of it. The doors to the houses did not have any bolts or locks. There was nothing to protect. Because of this, it was dangerous to stay at one place for a long time.

As I walked from place to place, people collecting toddy and potters had seen me. Even though I was travelling incognito and dressed differently, I felt afraid. I would feel that I would not make it to the next village. At such times, the children did an important job. They would follow the men and inform us about their doings. This made our work easier.

I had to make the entire journey on foot. It was impossible to use a bullock cart. While on foot, it was easy to slip away and hide from the road if we saw somebody coming or got news that someone was coming that way. It would be difficult to do that when travelling in a bullock cart. Moreover, the passing of a bullock cart would be noticed and talked about more.

When we reached the next village, we found some people sitting in a circle with one person standing in the centre. It was a discussion over some questions of justice that had to be decided by the village council. It was an *Adivasi* custom to discuss a question and make a decision in this manner. The two sides implemented the decision and gave toddy to the arbiters of the village council.

After visiting 15 villages, holding meetings in some and talking to leaders in others, I reached Ankalas village in Umbargaon taluka. Considering the movements of the police and the atmosphere in the village, we decided to move on.

"We Were a Bit Lax . . ."

There is no jungle near Ankalas village. The only trees are toddy palms. We judged it unsafe to travel over open ground in daylight. So we decided to rest in a pandal in the fields far from the village. I had been travelling for 13 days. Most *Adivasis* in the area knew I was there. I wondered if the police would have got scent of it. Even if the population in general was loyal to the cause, it was not impossible that there was one traitor among them. Great struggles produce great leaders and workers but also traitors. We experienced this in 1951. A reward had been announced for my capture. An *Adivasi* who had come to meet me had given my location to the police for the reward money. Now, since there were no trees or mountains around, I had to spend the night in the open in the fields. I went to the pandal in the field. I spread the mat on the ground and lay down. I immediately fell asleep from the physical and mental fatigue.

Adivasis cooked the meal and woke me up when it was ready at around nine at night. I rinsed my mouth and ate a hearty meal of *bhakari* and whole *tuar* cooked with salt. *Adivasis* did not know about oil, spices, and seasoning or *tadka*. Even if some knew, they could not afford it. It was not advisable to hold a big meeting there. A few *Adivasis* from the surrounding villages had come there and sat smoking *bidis*. Someone brought cow's milk. It was winter and it was very cold in the field. We made tea with jaggery and drank it hot. It refreshed us. The discussions went on until one in the morning. We all slept around the fire that burned all night. A few *Adivasis* stayed awake to keep watch. They woke me up at three in the morning. Due to extreme fatigue, I had been careless travelling that day. I could not get up. Finally at four the *Adivasis* urged me to get up and start on my way. As the tea things had been used up the previous night, I just rinsed my mouth and left. That day, I hated having to go on. But if I had not left, I would definitely have been caught. I began to walk without complaint. The journey was difficult. It was cold and dark and the road seemed never to end. The grass had not been cut. The dew made it wet and my *chappals* slipped on it. If I took off the *chappals*, the small stones on the path dug into the soles of the feet, sometimes very painfully. *Adivasis* asked me to meet somebody or the other at the houses on the way and so it was seven in the morning and quite light by the time we reached Bhilad village. I realised how lax I had been. But it was no use crying over spilt milk. It was flat ground all around and only a few trees, which could not give cover. I began to think that I would be caught and arrested if I was on that open ground in broad daylight. I did not want my guides to be arrested with me and asked them to go back. After having travelled successfully for 14 days, I was going to be arrested because of my own negligence. The thought pained made me and brought tears to my eyes. I thought of how the workers would feel, how it would hurt Comrade Parulekar, and how it would affect the struggle.

The *Adivasi* in whose home I stayed in Bhilad village was unaware of the danger in my staying there. He was very happy to receive me. After taking the tea he made of grass rather than tea leaves, I gave him an idea of how things stood. He started to think. Many Dhodi and Dubale *Adivasis* had been there to meet me. Bhilad police station was near that hamlet. It would not have taken long for the news to reach there. It was dangerous to walk in broad daylight. But it was even more dangerous to remain in the hut. I could attempt to leave only because of the *Adivasis*' support and their knowledge of escape routes. I wore a disguise and left for Borlai village with a child. We walked avoiding the farmers in the fields, the toddy makers, and the supervisors, stopping sometimes and hastening at others, and made it to Borlai at half past nine or ten in the morning.

Some farmers had probably heard that I was going to Borlai. They ran to intercept me on the way to have a few words with me. They would tell me the safer path to take. I had planned to eat something and rest at Borlai and then continue on. I sat down on a cot under a tree. I had had some jaggery tea in the morning. As tea was being prepared, I asked after the families of the *Adivasis* who were in jail.

"Who is She? Woman Back From in-Laws' Home!"

But I was not destined to have tea there. My carelessness cost me. I was lying on the cot when a supervisor came by. My throat went dry. In *Adivasi* areas, if one raised one's voice, these people would be cowed down. I raised my voice and asked him in Gujarati, "Why are you here?" He replied, "To cut grass." I shot back, "There is no grass here. Leave immediately." He went away. But I thought he might have gone to the police station. My doubt turned out to be correct. I got up as soon as he left. Forget the tea! The border to the foreign area, meaning Nagarhaveli, was two miles from where I was. *Adivasis* advised me to go there. The police did not go to the area where there were no *Adivasi* hamlets. We decided I should go to a place where I was not likely to meet anyone who knew me. Since the *Adivasis* knew the territory well, their advice could not be wrong. I left trusting their advice. I wore a black *sari* with a red border and draped it in the Gujarati manner and covered my face with the *pallu*. A Warli accompanied me carrying my dirty cloth bundle on his head. He walked ahead of me. The grass land owners and supervisors were standing at many places along the way. We did not say a word. If anybody asked about me, the Warli would reply that I was a married woman back from her in-laws' home. It was plausible since it was the time of Diwali and women often travelled between the married and natal homes. When I sensed somebody on the right, I looked to the left, and if I heard somebody on the left, I turned my face to the right. The *Adivasis*' guess turned to be correct. On the way, one person asked, "Who is she?" The Warli answered, "Back from in-laws' home." We slipped ahead. At such times, the road seems unending. Finally, when there was no one around, I ran. At last, we reached the Nagarhaveli boundary. There were only thorny trees and open ground. There was no shade and no water anywhere close by. My watch was in the bundle, but I didn't want to take it out and see the time. What was the use? It was necessary to continue the journey and reach the next destination. We rested for some time and then started walking again. We walked through muddy ground on the way. We crossed the streams and brooks, and our feet throbbed from walking on the stones.

At noon or about one in the afternoon, I reached the banks of Banaganga river on the border of Thane district. What do I see! Some 15-20 *Adivasi* chiefs from Borlai and other villages had gathered there to meet me. They had been worried about me. They were eagerly waiting to see me safe. I was moved by their determination, concern for me, and indifference to their own safety. I forgot all about missing tea that morning.

While I was there, the magistrate was touring the region to talk to *Adivasis* and persuade them. *Adivasis* boycotted the tour. My enthusiasm doubled as a result. There was no knowing when the police would come and arrest me. So I gave only the most important instructions and left immediately. I was going to cross the Banganga river and enter Surat district. The monsoon had just ended; the river was swollen and the current was strong. I could not have crossed the river on my own. With two *Adivasis*, I entered the water at a shallow spot. My feet started to slip on the smooth stones. The *Adivasis* gripped me on either side. They tied my luggage over the head and helped me to cross waist-high water. I went to Lavachha village on the other side. The people of that village had heard about me. I changed into dry clothes. It was almost time for the bus to Vapi station and I started for the bus stop.

I heaved a sigh of relief when I reached Vapi station. After 15 days, I stood at a tea stall a free person not hiding from anybody and greedily drank two cups of real tea. Once I boarded the passenger train to Mumbai, I felt the effects of walking eight to ten miles and running two to four furlongs. I had not eaten a morsel of food since morning. My feet were swollen. I could not wait to reach home.

Around eight at night I reached my house in the western suburb of Khar. Comrade Parulekar and Comrade Godiwala were anxiously waiting for me. Comrade Godiwala saw me and exclaimed, "So you have finally arrived." I was so exhausted and excited that I could neither eat nor sleep. We talked for a long time about the events of the past 15 days. Comrade Parulekar was a man of few words, but his eyes expressed his happiness and his pride in me. I slept the whole of the next day. I dreamt of lions, tigers, the jungle, and chases. My legs were swollen and I could not open my eyes. On the third day the exhaustion subsided and I returned to the world of human beings.

"Trees and Stones are Also on Your Side!"

I had not appreciated the alertness with which *Adivasis* had watched over me. They were prepared to carry on the struggle for many days. But they wanted our decision on whether the organisation they had built and the steps they had taken were right or wrong. My going there had made them feel better. Landlords had taunted them saying, "Where is your Madam? The government has put her in jail." They took pride in the fact that their Madam had come, they had met her, and they had protected her. They had confirmation that the landlords were lying. No matter how much the landlords derided them, *Adivasis* never made the mistake of replying, "Madam is here and she met us." Their behaviour with the landlords expressed, "Say what you will, one day you will know the truth." Some *Adivasis* would lose patience. When the landlords said, "We have driven out Madam" they would reply, "The lady is in Mumbai and also in the jungle. One day she is in jail and one day in the jungle." At this, the landlords would be dismissive, "What stupid people these are." When they learnt the truth, they would say, "What sly people. They never let on." The attitude underlying their behaviour was their contempt for the poor *Adivasis*.

I toured the villages for 15 days in spite of the repressive actions of the government. I do not remember with certainty what villages I visited nor the route. This 15-day tour over a 100 miles had a very favourable impact on *Adivasis*. It gave a boost to their courage and their confidence in the Communist Party. The entire community was filled with emotion. We saw again the magic of faith in the cause.

During my tour, news that I was in the area spread like wildfire. Women and children were asking "Has Madam really come?" Whatever they learnt working on the fields, homes, and villages of the landlords, they conveyed to me in minute detail. The youngsters acting as shepherds told me about the movements of government officers. They ran carrying messages of danger or giving the all clear. If *Adivasis* ran into me while travelling, they never gave any signs of recognition. Some came to talk to me at night. Not everyone could meet me. But my visit was a balm to them during this time of terrible suffering.

In the presence of the landlords, *Adivasis* pretended ignorance of the red flag and acted petrified. However much government officials abused or threatened them, they kept an unemotional, expressionless face and pretended a state of utter ignorance. Landlords and moneylenders would beat them to find out the truth, but that did not help.

At the time of the struggle for the liberation of Nagarhaveli, I was in Ughava village in Umbargaon taluka. I was 50 yards from where the police superintendent of Thane district camped with his force. My home was watched day and night by armed policemen posted every ten feet. Every morning, the superintendent did an inspection under the pretext of calling on me. I told him that 21 people had entered the village of Nagarhaveli through this cordon. He replied, "The trees, flowers, and fruits, the cattle, the stones and boulders, the children—they are all known to you. They talk to you. The people are with you. What can people like us do here? We can break our heads but achieve nothing."

He was right. That is what I experienced in my 15-day tour. I moved about that area like a fish in the ocean. For 15 days, I travelled in that area through the police security and the landlords' watchdogs, and won the hearts of the *Adivasis*, and then safely returned to Mumbai.

XII

Let Bygones be Bygones

The heroic struggle of the *Adivasis* transformed the society of that area. As the *Adivasi* community changed, so did the stance of the landlords and moneylenders and the middle class.

In 1945, just as *Adivasis* were very backward so were the landlords. Although their children studied at colleges in Mumbai and Pune, it had no effect on their lives and culture. They firmly believed that the culture, thinking, and ideas of the city were for the city; that it was a different world; that in the villages everything would remain the same. Their life was tradition-bound and narrow. Only a few of them had participated in the freedom struggle.

The landlords were Hindu—Marathi, Gujarati, Marwari, and North Indians—Parsi, Irani, and Muslim. Most of them were members of the landed gentry and lived very similar social lives.

Hindu and Muslim landlords had large old-style houses. The houses had a few wooden chairs and a bench. The seating was mainly old-fashioned mattresses, cushions, rugs, and carpets on the floor. There would be a swing in an inner room or on the veranda. Parsi and Irani landlords had more luxurious lifestyles. Some of them embraced a western lifestyle. Their houses had tables, chairs, heavy couches, and a lot of old furniture. They lived in huge old-fashioned bungalows. But they were no different in exploitation. One Parsi landlord used to take a chicken at the price of an egg. When asked why he did it, he would say, "I had given him the egg which has hatched into this chicken, so I am paying the price of an egg." They got milk, ghee, vegetables, and food for free so there was no scarcity nor any need to worry about daily expenses. They never had to do any physically strenuous work. Most had a poor relation staying with them who would do all the farm work. Other than accounts and some supervision, the landlords had little to do. Because there was almost no work, they had a lot of free time on their hands.

Even in rich homes, the kitchenware was usually discoloured from cooking fires and well water. As firewood was free, most used wood-burning *chulhas* or rarely kerosene stoves.

Their topics of conversation were limited. Hindu landlords sat on their verandas drinking tea several times a day and chewing paan and betel nut or tobacco. Parsi and Irani landlords sat chatting in chairs or on benches. Their reading did not go beyond a Marathi or Gujarati newspaper.

Conversations often centred on food. If there had been a feast for a happy occasion or a death in the village, the food would be discussed with relish. There they sat on the swings, wearing a *dhoti*, with one leg drawn up and giving a gentle push to the swing with the other, and talked about brinjal vegetable and spicy *vaal* for hours. If a farmer had vegetables in his home, they would discuss if the farmer had delivered them to their houses. One of their special customs was to celebrate the festival of Holi by making potato snacks and coffee on the Holi bonfire.

The tours of collectors or police superintendents, and the visits of police officers, district magistrates, or forest officers were topics of great interest. Landlords made considerable effort to maintain good relationships with all these.

The third topic of interest was *Adivasi* women. Landlords saw nothing wrong in teasing each other about their relationships with *Adivasi* women. Maintaining a concubine was considered a prerogative of wealth and social status. Nobody felt disgust or regret at it.

Earnings from the land, grass, and jungle were topics of conversation as were *Adivasis*. They would narrate in detail how an *Adivasi* had overstepped his limits and how he was whipped and brought to heel. Sitting on the swing, they would entertain themselves by threatening *Adivasis* with whips and flinging foul and obscene abuses at them. They believed that obscene and coarse language was the right language to talk to the poor. They were not civilised enough to know that, when a person beats a fellow human being, the assaulter is diminished not the victim.

I used to be surprised that among them were lawyers, law graduates, and barristers. Class interest had engulfed their culture and education. Some of the children of the landlords were lawyers or doctors and worked in the cities at well-paid jobs or businesses. But they, too, abused Warlis and extracted vegetables on their visits. I sometimes wondered if it was something in the air of the place! But it is the nature of class conflict that the exploiter loses all humanity.

Their concept of culture was orthodox and regressive. They cared nothing about the new society being created, modern culture, international politics, poverty of the masses, or their betterment. Their views on culture and social life were different from contemporary ones. Public life in their areas was like a stagnant pool of water. That smooth, unchallenged life of luxury received a jolt when *Adivasis* brought the red flag from Titwala.

Landlords did not think much of it at first. But when *Adivasis* began to win one demand after another with the help of the red flag, the Communist Party, democratically minded public, and progressive politicians, landlords were forced to sit up and take notice. They were forced to take notice of things beyond their world.

Retreat of Landlords and Moneylenders

District collector Bedekar taught landlords and moneylenders their first lesson. After October 10, 1945, Bedekar held a meeting of landlords in Homi Daviyarwala's bungalow at Sanjan. In summary, he said: "This is 1945 and the Second World War has ended. You must understand the changes occurring around the world and change your attitude towards *Adivasis*."

The collector left the meeting. The landlords were displeased with him. They felt that *Adivasis* were at fault for forgetting their station and yet the collector had chided them. They expressed their displeasure in loud and aggressive comments. Comrade Parulekar was sitting there. He listened to their discussion. We were there because Bedekar had called us for a meeting on the same day. I had gone to the upper floor first. Comrade Parulekar had been on the ground floor and followed me up a little later. None of the landlords knew him. Besides, they were too angry to notice him. They saw nothing wrong or reprehensible in the way they treated *Adivasis*. Their conversation showed us the need for the advice the district collector had given them.

Landlords had two strategies. The first was to harass me until I left. The second was to thrash *Adivasis* until they gave in. Their plan was to spend some money to hire a few thugs and have them beat *Adivasis*. To get the government's support, they made a request that while the beatings went on, the government should stay away and not intervene. The landlords were backward enough to think that the recently elected national government would disregard the progressive leaders and the democratic aspirations of the public and give them permission for such activities.

They described their plans in a meeting of major landlords in Umbargaon held to discuss the struggle for a united Maharashtra. They were disappointed that the government did not approve their plan as it was.

I remember an incident at Sanjan station. I was sitting in the waiting room waiting for the passenger train to Mumbai. A Parsi landlord's wife came in gasping for breath. She hugged me and pleaded, "I am a poor woman. Do not stop my work with bonded labour. You are a woman. I am sure you will care about me." I told her, "Precisely because I am a woman I see it as my duty to care about the starving *Adivasi* women and their children. You too should do that and pay them fair wages for work." She did not immediately understand what I had said and stared at me. When she understood, she and her thugs started gesticulating angrily and abusing me. They had already forgotten that I too was a woman.

When I stood on a station platform, the landlords and their hangers-on would gesticulate and talk. They would point to me and laugh. They would make dirty noises and sing songs. Once they sent a drunk to scare me. They had done all they could to ensure that in their villages we would not get a place for an office, no one would give us rooms and not even a drink of water.

We heard that in one of their meetings, somebody had put forward the suggestion of having Comrade Dalvi and I killed.

They assumed that things would be easier if they could scare me away or eliminate me. The Communist Party, its politics, its style of functioning, and its objectives were all new to the landlords. They did not understand that the ideology could not be destroyed by such means.

After the firing of 1945, landlords steadily retreated. *Adivasis* won their demands one after another. The tenancy farming law was amended to abolish the system of paying the landlord's share in produce. The amended law provided that the landlords' share would be paid in money and at the rate of five times the land tax or 20 rupees per acre. The newly awakened *Adivasis* got these legal concessions implemented with the help of Kisan Sabha and Communist Party workers. That opened the landlords' eyes. The fact that the government had been compelled to accept *Adivasis*' demands showed them which way the winds of change were blowing. The reality of a power greater than landlords eroded their prestige, position, and power in rural society. As *Adivasis* got the legal concessions implemented, the exploitative structure was uprooted. The relationship between the landlord and the *Adivasi* changed a little.

The class-conscious *Adivasi* organisation froze the abusive language on the landlords' lips. The hands that had raised a whip shook. Boasts of teaching a lesson subsided.

Adivasis described this change in landlords' and moneylenders' behaviour in an amusing way: "Moneylender has grown soft. He couldn't speak to us without swearing. Now he says, 'Navshyadada, how are you?' " Government officials changed in similar ways. Civil officials and police personnel started greeting *Adivasis* politely and the swearing stopped.

Earlier, when *Adivasis* went to landlords' houses for any work, they would stand in the courtyard outside or squat in a corner with their heads bowed. After the awakening, landlords invited those same *Adivasis*, "Come, Devaji, come up here. Sit here. Why are you sitting down?" *Adivasis* would reply, "No, Seth. I am fine down here." Inwardly the *Adivasi* would smile and know that those who had boasted of throwing out the red flag had been straightened out by the red flag. *Adivasis* understood why the landlords were being so polite. They enjoyed telling me of such incidents. Landlords were prepared to retreat on certain points considering the situation. But this was not an indication of any change of heart. It was only an admission of defeat before the strength of the *Adivasi* organisation.

Landlords and moneylenders had perpetrated atrocities on *Adivasis* through their henchmen. These men were usually poor relations living in the landlords' household. When the machinery of exploitation collapsed, these henchmen were rendered useless. The landlords soon forgot that before 1945 these people had obeyed their every word and done their bidding. They were now a burden on the landlords. These men who had basked in reflected glory now became helpless and their attitude changed.

"We Did Not Understand—Forgive Us!"

In Khattalwad village in Umbargaon taluka, Virkar had lived in landlord Pimputkar's household. Virkar wore rings on all his fingers, walked around the village threatening people with a stick, and had warned everyone against giving me a place to stay. When we next met Virkar after 1953, he was in an outer room in Pimputkar's house, bedridden and lying there unwanted. When Comrade Parulekar and I went to meet him in his last days, he said with tears in his eyes, "When I opposed you, I did not understand. Forgive me. If I survive, I will work with you in your party." Comrade Parulekar was such a sensitive and generous person that when a person apologised in such an abject manner, he felt embarrassed. He took Virkar's hand in his own hands and said a few words of solace and we left. We were both silent for some time.

Mama Mukadam was the maternal uncle of the landlord Dhapare. He looked after the landlord's properties. He changed so much in 1952 that he was elected to the district board with the support of the Communist Party. I got the news of his election on Party support when I was in jail. I could not believe it at first; it was so unexpected. I was baffled at this change. There were many such examples.

We shared in the success of the *Adivasis*. After the *Adivasi* victory, when landlords started ill-treating their now-useless dependents, those dependents became curious about us. We had no personal animosity towards them. They started to come to us and began to change.

In the state elections of 1952, Comrade Shidawa Sapata and I were the Communist Party candidates. We had gone to Dahanu from the jail under police escort for the counting of votes. Barjor came to meet us, the same Barjor who had been infamous during the struggle for beating people with the help of the police. I refused to talk to him. Comrade Shidawa told me, "Madam, talk to him. I have definite information that he has changed." The behaviour of many people changed in this way. At one time, the district Communist Party representatives lived in Dhapare's house in Khattalwad.

The small and medium landlords underwent a change at this time. The law on bonded labour was applicable to all landlords. The impact on the big, rich landlords was minor. But the small and medium landlords lost their source of livelihood. They had neither the strength nor the organisational unity to put up resistance and their condition became pitiable.

During the period of *Adivasis'* troubles and our ostracism, these small landlords had never sided with us against the big landlords. The rich helped them and they were under their influence. Under the new circumstances, when the influence of the landlords began to wane, the small landlords wanted to talk to us. But they could not muster the courage to do so. They were embarrassed. When we started talking to them without reservations, they were surprised. We started interacting with them. As they understood our stand, the distance between us narrowed. Not only that, they felt a kind of warmth for us. Some landlords ceased to see us as untouchables. They realised that there was a big force and they had to recognise it.

The prestige and position the Communist Party achieved in this area after 1953 was due, besides the masses, to the tireless work of Comrade Laxman Bapu Dhanagar, Comrade BM Narvekar, Comrade Dhakat Sutar, Comrade Rock Carvalho, Comrade Dnyaneshwar Dere, Comrade Haribhau Virkar, Comrade Ramakant Gupte, Comrade Rupaji Kadu, Comrade Lahanu Kom, Comrade Vadhan, and many other Adivasi Party workers who were loyal, sacrificing, idealistic, and worked day and night with great determination.

In this changed environment, the movement for a united Maharashtra started. A meeting was called in 1953 in Thane district to prepare for the federation for a United Maharashtra. I announced that thousands of *Adivasis* would attend the meeting and the atmosphere changed. At a meeting in Shirgaon a few days later, the landlords said, "What flowed was the Ganga and what remains is the sanctified water," in other words, let bygones be bygones. They expressed a desire for compromise. In this environment, there was free and frank discussion.

As I write this today, it pricks at my heart that 16 contiguous Marathi-speaking villages in Umbargaon taluka were not included in Maharashtra. I will continue to feel it until these 16 villages are included in Maharashtra.

The Communist party held big rallies in Thane district at this time, which were attended by thousands. In these rallies, I gave detailed information about *Adivasi* struggle and explained our point of view. Misunderstandings about us were removed. Our status as untouchables ended. We formed warm relationships with many middle class people. Some people began to say, "This woman has entered our homes, all the way to the kitchen. She has won our sympathy." Others said, "This is a simple woman. People were speaking nonsense about her." So, with the success of *Adivasi* struggle, we developed affectionate relations with people.

It is time now for everyone to say let bygones be bygones and unite the exploited poor farmers and farm labourers, bring them together with the middle class, and, under the leadership of the labour class, work to eliminate poverty and give power to the exploited. I do not think that I would be privileged to see it happen. I am confident that the exploited class and history will do their appointed task. That is the law of history. There will be obstacles in the path. Stones and thorns will bleed the feet. But the struggle will go on. The Ganga never flows backwards.

XIII

Meeting the Outside World

Adivasis had been cut off from the rest of the society. Nobody had ever told them that they had anything to do with the outside world and that they would eventually integrate into that world. *Adivasis*' interaction with the world was in very basic matters. Their vocabulary was limited. They never felt the need for more words. They made do with a few words and simple sentences. They had no conception of punctuality as it is understood in a city. If I missed a bus leaving a village, they would say, "So what? You missed it today, but you will get it tomorrow." Today and tomorrow were the same to them.

Many times they appeared for a court hearing the next day or two day later; they came saying they were there for the court date. They gave no importance to punctuality or the passage of time. They had never needed these concepts. Only in relation to farming activities did they care about time. It was a necessity of their life. It was imperative to perform farm work on time. They took the pleasure of creative work in growing crops. They have recently begun to appreciate the importance of time and punctuality because they now attend Communist Party and Kisan Sabha meetings and rallies.

As their life was slow paced, they spoke very slowly. They took time grasping what we said. Sometimes I would joke, "It takes time for what enters the ears to reach your head and be understood, does it?" Landlords and moneylenders always shouted at them and so they did not understand something said in a normal tone. One had to shout to make sure they understood. Initially, when a meeting ended, they would not get up until the shouted announcement "Get up. The meeting is over." Living in fear had become such an ingrained habit that their faces expressed no emotions, neither sadness nor joy.

In the early days, when we made speeches before *Adivasis*, we floundered badly. In the first six months, Comrade Parulekar and I made many speeches but never knew how much they understood and how much went over their heads. They understood about landlords, moneylenders, exploitation, atrocities, and the need for unity. It was their direct experience. But they understood little of other topics.

"Madam, the Heart Knows."

I vividly recall one incident regarding Warli education. At the Zari rally, I asked four or five intelligent Warlis to stay overnight. We decided to talk to them the next day about the basic tenets of Communism and the Communist Party.

The next day I started a study session with those four or five Warlis. I started by telling them what is meant by 'society'. I was trying to explain class relations, production relations, and class struggle. Soon Comrade Rupaji Kadu yawned, leant against the wall and dozed. His face was so blank that I lost heart, lost my enthusiasm for teaching. The others also started dozing. I was nonplussed. Crestfallen, I wrapped up the class. In the next two to three years, this same Comrade Rupaji Kadu became a loyal, aware, and thinking Party worker and leader. He made excellent speeches to thousands of people in rallies.

I remember an illuminating example of how our speeches went over the people's heads in the early days of the movement. We often used the word 'colonialism' in our speeches. I often felt that our audience did not know the meaning of this word. One day I asked a young Warli, "What is colonialism? Tell me what you understand by the word?" He was silent for a moment and then guessed, "It must be something like landlordism, something against us." I was amused by his guesswork and said, "Oh Surji, even this word gives trouble. We have used this word so many times. What can we do! How can we teach you?" He was a little dejected at my words, but quickly replied, "How could we understand, Madam? We have never heard this word. This word is never spoken in the landlords' houses. How are we to know the word when we have never heard it?" His reply was not only correct but also shrewd. It was true that the landlords and moneylenders of that time were similarly ignorant. I could not explain the meaning of colonialism in a way he would understand.

We then made a list of the words often used in political speeches. We then deliberated on how to explain these words. We discussed this amongst ourselves and with the *Adivasis*. We outlined how to explain words in everyday use that have a special meaning in political terminology. We conducted study sessions to explain these words. In addition, whenever we stayed in villages, we talked about it. After hearing these words regularly, *Adivasis* began to recognise them. In a few days, they started to understand the meanings. Now they use them correctly.

Comrade Parulekar, I, and many Party workers held innumerable meetings in this area. We stayed in almost all the villages. We spent whole nights talking to the poor people about politics in a language they could understand. A non-English speaking person, after staying many days in an English-speaking home, begins to understand and speak the language. Similarly, the *Adivasis*, through frequent contact with us and our conscious efforts, started to understand and even speak politics. They made rapid progress because of their keen desire to learn new things and our well-thought-out efforts.

Comrade Parulekar and I began work determined to bring humanity to this backward community and to awaken them politically. After some time, we saw a change in the community. When a Warli stood on the podium and made a political speech or suggested good tactics during a discussion, it gave us great pleasure. Many such workers have been created in the past 20 years.

Even when the *Adivasis* understood what we said, they could not explain what they had understood. We would ask them questions to gauge whether they had understood. They could not answer and felt bad about it. Then one of them explained their problem, "Madam, our heart understands, but we cannot say it." He meant that they understood and imbibed what was said but could not express it in words. Later, as the habit of using words developed, some *Adivasis* began to give the right answers.

In 1955, we conducted political study sessions or classes for 300 *Adivasis*. Comrade Narvekar and Comrade Dhanagar organised these classes for selected comrades. Whenever Comrade Parulekar and I went to a village for a public meeting, we went in the morning. We would call the chief comrades from nearby villages and conduct classes. Many *Adivasis* learnt about politics in these classes. Comrade Parulekar would ask questions after a lecture. *Adivasis* found it difficult to answer. One would give an excuse such as "My throat is aching. I can't speak." Others would get up to drink water or smoke *bidis*. They were trying to avoid answering the question. We would be amused at this childlike behaviour in grown-ups. After some time, they would try to answer. Once the ice was broken, they would start talking among themselves. They would decide on an answer and one of them would give it. The study sessions had to have *bidi* breaks of 15 minutes every hour or hour and a half. They could not concentrate if made to sit for two to three hours at a stretch. Even today, if we explain something that requires concentration, it should not be explained for longer than an hour and a half. This is their intellectual capacity. They cannot bear more mental strain. They start yawning. Their faces show that they would not understand anything explained from then on.

Adivasi Horizons Have Widened

At Mahalakshmi village in Dahanu taluka, Comrade Parulekar conducted two-day study sessions for about 3,000 farmers. People bought their own food with them. In those two days, many *Adivasis* understood new ideas and gained a new perspective on issues close to their hearts. They were so happy that they gathered around Comrade Parulekar at the end of the second day before leaving for their homes. They did not know how to express their joy, love, and respect. They gathered around him and just kept looking at him.

I always started the lectures. After I made a speech, Comrade Parulekar's ideas would flow easily. He insisted that I speak first. If I did not speak first, he would not speak. He was so adamant about it that if I did not start, he would refuse to speak. I always had to give in and start the sessions.

Some landlords and their collaborators would tell *Adivasis*, "The red flag talks nonsense to you. The government has the power and the army. How can you take the lands?" *Adivasis* retorted, "Even when the government had the power and the army, we abolished bonded labour and reduced crop shares. We will take back our lands in the same way." The answer angered the landlords, but they said okay and withdrew without arguing further.

It was difficult to explain anything to *Adivasis.* They knew nothing of taluka, district, state, nation, and the world. It needed immense effort to explain to them international unity of the working class. I had a 10 ft × 6 ft world map that I shaded in two colours to show two types of countries. I would put up this map in every public meeting and explain it. Gradually they started to develop an idea of the world. In our office, we had maps of India, Maharashtra, and various districts, which we explained to them. With that, *Adivasis* knew about India.

Travel helped greatly in widening *Adivasis'* horizons and improving their understanding and experience. When emergency had been declared in Thane district and all our workers had been expelled from the district, the 1947 Thane Party conference had to be held at the Blavatsky Lodge in Mumbai. Two hundred *Adivasis* came to Mumbai to attend that conference.

Many *Adivasis* travelled to Dhule, Jalgaon, Nagar, Nashik, Pune, and other cities as delegates and audience members for state and district conferences. Party members from different districts had an opportunity to get to know one another. *Adivasis* who had not thought beyond their villages started talking with fellow-feeling about *Adivasis* in other districts. They developed warm feelings towards other *Adivasi* communities and became aware of the spread of their own community. They met non-*Adivasi* farmers of Maharashtra. For the All India Kisan Sabha conference, they went to places like Gazipur, Moha, Mayavaram, and Trichur. Travel helped many *Adivasis* lose their narrow-mindedness, widen their horizons, and increase the scope of their idea of unity.

Adivasis did not know amounts such as thousand, lakh, and crore. They were used to counting the bales of grass they had cut. Five bundles made one bale (*ganji*), 500 bundles made a larger bale (*ganj*), and that was one lakh of grass—some understood this calculation. They did not understand crore. In their daily lives, there was no need of it. When numbers were explained with reference to their transactions, they started to understand. We always tried to explain everything to them with reference to their lives.

The awareness that they belonged among lakhs of party members around the world and were part of the effort to eliminate exploitation throughout the world made them proud. When they were told that Communist party members worldwide numbered in crores, they were eager to understand 'crore'. To understand it, they took two heaps of grain and started counting. But they soon tired of it. After counting for a while, they had a general idea and gave up counting.

There is no doubt that Warlis learnt a great many invaluable ideas in a short time during their unparalleled struggle. The constant companionship of many Party workers also made an important contribution to their education. The political awareness and organisation of Warlis today owes to the efforts of many workers. They gave their all to build the organisation. This cannot be achieved merely by going on tours, making speeches, doing spot visits, and organising study sessions once or twice a year. It has to be done by living in the villages and gaining direct experience. Today the political awareness of *Adivasis* is better developed than many other farmers considered educated, progressive, modern, and cultured.

Adivasis wanted to know more than landlords and moneylenders. Many a times, when the supposedly ignorant *Adivasis* spoke, even the landlords were silenced.

In this way, *Adivasis* who had forgotten they were human because their humanity had been destroyed by the landlords, who lay apathetic from the landlords' atrocities and starvation—those same *Adivasis* awoke once they were brought out of their isolated existence in the villages and given a broader outlook. They gained confidence from organisation and their capacity to resist. They regained pride. The Warli who came through the trial by fire of the struggle and was shaped by the movement was a fundamentally changed class-conscious Warli. The education and experience that would normally take years were acquired in just days during the struggle. He understood that others enjoyed the wealth created by him while he starved. He began to say, "I will not die of starvation."

"What Magic Did You Do?"

During the struggle, many *Adivasis* had been held in police lock-up for some reason or the other. Cases had been filed against them. After the firing of 1945, I often attended court to give support to *Adivasis* or to get them released on bail. I spent entire days in criminal or civil courts. In the court premises, hordes of farmers would be waiting. It gave me a chance to meet farmers from different villages. While doing this, I saw amusing examples of how *Adivasis* had changed.

One afternoon I was walking from Mule's house to the district court in Umbargaon. Generally, no educated person in Umbargaon talked to us. To them, we were untouchables.

That day, a bespectacled elderly white collar man suddenly appeared in front of me and said, "What magic have you done? *Adivasis* used to tremble at the prospect of merely standing before the magistrates. They would be speechless. We had seen this for years. Now they give forthright answers. Forget the constable, they are not even afraid of the magistrate. Even when the magistrate was a big landlord, they gave confident answers. What have you done to them?" This man worked at the district court. I did not understand what he said at first. But when I asked, he told me the whole story.

Many *Adivasis* were held in the Umbargaon lock-up. Among them was a bold young man. One day the magistrate visited the lock-up. He stood just outside the lock-up gates and tried to explain things to Warlis. A magistrate coming to speak to them was an entirely new experience for *Adivasis*. The magistrate told a youth called Jethya to give up the folly of the red flag and the struggle and dangled the carrot of a good job. He explained why it was better to take a good job and enjoy an easy life than to follow the red flag and languish in jail. Jethya heard him out and then replied, "How long will the government keep us in jail? A year or two. But they will release us someday. When we gain power, these prisons will be useful to lock you up."

The landlord-magistrate was stunned at this reply from an illiterate, half-naked *Adivasi*. This farmer's reply was not only unexpected but also insulting to the Seth. He turned back. The man who told me the story said that the rest of the court staff were equally astonished to hear this reply from the Warli. The man added, "I happened to see you and could not but talk to you. I had to tell you what I have personally seen and heard. I would never have believed it if someone had told me such a story. That is why I asked you what magic have you done?" The magic was not done by me but by Marxism and the Communist Party. The man could not imagine how much and how quickly a society could change during a revolutionary struggle. This incident is engraved in my mind.

Courageous Retaliation

Adivasis who had seen government officials and especially police officials as the embodiment of state power, made a police sub-inspector void a *panchanama* he had conducted.

Some *Adivasis* of Rayatali had drunk toddy and were returning from Dahanu to Rayatali. Drunk on toddy, they were walking in the middle of the road. A landlord's tonga approached from behind them. On seeing Warlis in the middle of the road, the landlord swore as usual and asked them to move aside. The Warlis were angered by the abusive language. They stopped the tonga and, fuelled by the toddy, rebuked the landlord in no uncertain terms. After some more swearing on both sides, they let the tonga go. The landlord and his relative decided to avenge this insult. They filed a false complaint of theft of 50 rupees against the *Adivasis* and went to Rayatali with a police sub-inspector in tow.

They barged into a Warli house to search it. People gathered outside the house. The landlord's relative was standing outside the house. He quietly slipped a packet of five 10-rupee notes under the roof just above the doors. When the police sub-inspector and the landlord came out of the house, he showed them the bundle of money. The sub-inspector wrote a *panchanama* or report to the effect that stolen property had been found. By then many *Adivasis* had gathered. When the sub-inspector wrote and read out the *panchanama*, the *Adivasis* showed their new face. Some people had seen the relative slip the bundle of money under the roof. They said loud and clear that the *panchanama* was false. Things reached a point where the sub-inspector had to hand over the false *panchnama* to the *Adivasis* and go back to Dahanu empty-handed.

Adivasis wanted the *panchanama* so that they could give it to the Communist Party office as evidence of landlords' falsehoods and deception.

The landlord and the government officials did not give up. They filed a complaint of robbery against the *Adivasis*. The next morning, the superintendent of police Sharif Khan went to Rayatali with a police force, arrested 55 *Adivasis* who were inconvenient to the landlord, and took them to Dahanu. I was shocked at the news of the arrest of 55 people. The problem was how to arrange the thousands needed to bail out so many people. I had to consider the possible effect on *Adivasis* of being thrown into jail for no reason and how the landlords might take advantage of the situation.

Comrade Parulekar and I puzzled over it. Telegrams from lawyers started pouring in asking for money for the bail. *Adivasis* held on to the hope that Madam would do something for them. When we could not see a way out, we went to Comrade Chandrakant Vaidya's home in Thane. Our problem was solved immediately there. His father Shridharpant Vaidya agreed to stand surety. That made it possible to have all the *Adivasis* released on bail. The movement proved useful. We could not find words to express our gratitude to Shridharpant. Ever since then, whenever the Rayatali incident was mentioned, Comrade Parulekar remembered Vaidya with gratitude. After a few months, all 55 *Adivasis* were acquitted of the charges. They came home shouting slogans in honour of the red flag.

The awakened *Adivasis* put a stop to their exploitation by civil officials. Farmers need the land records called *saat-baara* from the records of the civil administration. The fee for *saat-baara* at that time was 9 paisa. Talathis gave these *saat-baara* documents. One such Talathi took advantage of people's need for the document and charged 10-12 rupees for each document and made 300 rupees. *Adivasis* caught him, made him bow before the red flag, and forced him to return the 300 rupees. *Adivasis* were now more aware and began to challenge illegal and exploitative practices.

While I was expelled from the district, *Adivasis* did not hesitate to pay back for the atrocities by the landlords on the strength of their unity.

One landlord was surrounded by *Adivasis* and made to take off his clothes and wear a loincloth. He was given a load to carry on his head. *Adivasis* stood in a circle around him. One *Adivasi* would call him over using the calls for a dog. Just as the landlord got to him, another *Adivasi* would make the same call. The landlord was made to walk back and forth with the load on his head. When he was tired and begged to be let go, *Adivasis* chided him, "See how tired you feel now. The load was not heavy. You made us walk miles with heavy loads. How do you think we felt then?" Then the *Adivasis* let him go. They did not harm a hair on his head. The landlord put on his clothes and walked away.

Adivasis never told me about this incident; I heard it from one of the landlord's supervisors. *Adivasis* did not think that I would approve of such an act. What reasonable person would argue that such acts are justified? But they are forgivable considering the brutal treatment *Adivasis* had suffered and their experience of bringing down even the cruel state power on the strength of unity.

During the period when all party workers had been expelled, there may have been a few cases of inappropriate actions. But do the landlords not bear responsibility for the acts because they had driven *Adivasis* in that direction?

Adivasis had not been aware that there was any such thing as the law. We taught them this. *Adivasis* won their economic demands through the struggle but also gained political awareness from facing the power of the state and the landlords. They became aware of their political rights. In the 1947 elections, there was no universal franchise. Even so, the day before voting, hundreds of *Adivasis* stationed themselves outside the polling booths in defiance of government orders. They were very hurt that not every adult had the right to vote.

Adivasis began to learn politics from our meetings and their own experience. They were presented with two flags and two political parties. It made them think, aroused their curiosity.

"Madam, Who is This Russia?"

When I stayed in a hut in a village, the chiefs from that village and the surrounding area would gather. They would talk to me smoking *bidis*. On one such night as we sat talking, a few came forward to say something special. They asked in a tone of posing an important question, "Tell us the truth. Madam, who is this Russia? Does he give you money?" I was very amused at this. They had wondered who this Russia was that was giving money to their Madam. I asked, "Who told you this?" They said, "Bhise master used to say so. So would the moneylender. Red flag is not ours but belongs to Russia. Madam gets money from Russia. Madam takes the money but does not give it to you." This told me where their question came from. I told them about Russia. Russian peasants and workers ended exploitation by landlordism and established a workers' government. To protect that state, they have formed an unbeatable army of peasants and workers just like them. I told them these and other things in a simple language. They listened very attentively to make sure they understood every word that I was saying. In the quiet night, they would ask me question after question, and I struggled to explain in a language they would understand. These discussions on many topics went on into the early hours of the morning. I would be very tired. When the cool breeze started to blow at dawn, I would say, "Friends, I am very tired now. I have work to do tomorrow. I want to sleep. You too should sleep." I would fall asleep within five minutes. Some people slept while others went on speaking until morning. I had spoken to many poor farmers in Umbargaon, Dahanu, Palghar, Javhar, and Vada talukas. Many nights I stayed up in this way to educate them.

Our opponents helped our propaganda. They said certain things with one intention. But it made *Adivasis* curious and they would ask us questions. We would explain the matters they raised. Our political views became known to many *Adivasis* and their political awareness improved.

In one of our nightly discussions, *Adivasis* asked a question that showed their interest and curiosity. The Kisan Sabha had decided to take a procession to the state assembly to press the demand to reduce the landlord's share of the crop. We were planning to take about 20,000 farmers to Mumbai. During my stay, some five or six

Adivasis came to me and said, "We will be walking to Mumbai and will stop on the way for rest. How far is Russia from there? Couldn't we go on to Russia?" They had probably been speaking among themselves for many days about going to Russia. They were disappointed that they could not go to Russia. After that, whenever I went to any village, Warlis would say, "Madam, tells us all about Russia."

An indication of how much Warlis' political awareness had increased was the self-respect they displayed in prison. On August 15, 1947, thousands of *Adivasis* were languishing in jails in Thane, Nashik, Yerawada, and Visapur. The inmates in these jails were served a sweet to celebrate freedom on August 15, 1947. *Adivasis* did not touch the sweet. Their portions had to be fed to animals. Officials from Thane jail told me this in 1951. The jail officials tried to convince them with many arguments, but they did not listen. The *Adivasis* said, "We are not thieves, robbers or criminals." They had been fighting for justice and the government had thrown them in jail and deprived them of their freedom. They did not want the sweet. Later they had gone on a fast demanding release. The government was in a quandary. *Adivasis* were given assurances, some sincere and some not, and made to break their fast.

I heard about the fast in the jail much later. *Adivasis* did not think it was important enough to tell me. When I asked, they told me, "We were dumped into jail for no reason, so we decided to fight and fought. It had to be done. Without it, the government would never have released us."

External Changes

As a goat does not protest when its neck is slit, *Adivasis* had bowed before landlords. They had no capacity to resist. Who taught them this method of fasting for a demand? Where did these Warlis from the jungle learn political lessons? Their experiences woke them up. Understanding of politics transformed their childlike awareness into political maturity. They leapt over many steps in political evolution and overtook the supposedly progressive farmer.

When their economic demands were granted, their economic condition improved a little. Their social conditions and relationships also underwent a radical change. The *Adivasis* who had returned from prison had grown radically in self-esteem. They changed even more.

Their appearance and their external life changed. Most people got rid of the topknot and grew their hair. Young and old Warlis discarded the loincloth and started wearing half pants, shirts, and coats. Some wore pyjamas and full pants. Women started wearing full-length *saris*. They began to buy good kitchenware. Brass or China cups and saucers appeared in homes. In some places, spoons replaced ladles made of coconut shells.

Adivasis began to regret that they could not read or write. They were eager to understand politics. They began to pour all their energies into trying to understand what we said. They could not learn enough. Wherever they went, they became observant and lived with self-respect.

And so the *Adivasi* changed—the *Adivasi* who had lived in the craggy hills and jungles, who was like a fish out of water in the cities, who had never eaten oil, milk, or buttermilk, who had never even heard of the red flag—that *Adivasi* had changed so much now that, with the red flag in his hand, he had the ambition of understanding world politics.

Adivasis would comment on their progress. They would say, "Madam, what were we like earlier. We knew nothing except moneylenders, beatings, debt, marriage, birth and death, and farming. We never knew about the world. Today we talk about the Communist Party, red flag rallies, Party meetings, what the Congress has done, what the red flag has done, which Congress leader says what, what do our people say, why am I poor, why are we hungry, how do we take our work forward, when are our study sessions, what should we say to people. If we go to the city, landlords and shopkeepers receive us respectfully. We discuss the news and talk about Russia, China, and America. We feel that the doors to the world have opened to us."

XIV

Present State of Adivasis

If it seems that, after *Adivasis* fought for increase in wages and solutions to their economic problems, their economic conditions must have improved and hunger must have ended, that is not the case. *Adivasis*' economic condition has not improved much. Even today, four months in a year they do not have enough to eat; they subsist on roots and leaves when they do not starve.

The main reason for this condition is that their basic problem is land. Until that is solved, their economic condition will not improve. After the implementation of the tenancy farming law, the landlords' share in the produce has come down. Some *Adivasis* have paid shares equivalent to the value of the land and need not pay shares any more. They are for all practical purposes owners of the land. But the *Adivasis*' land holdings are so small that the yield from them is insufficient for one family.

If the *Adivasis*' economic condition is to improve, the land held by landlords must be appropriated and distributed free among *Adivasis*. The law of tenancy farming interprets 'tilling the land' to include a landlord employing workers to till his land. This distorted definition of the owner tilling the land has enabled landlords to keep thousands of acres of land. Many landlords live and work in cities and all the work is done by labourers. These landlords, who never set foot on the land, do not need the earning from the land. It is an injustice to let them keep the land. Only the landlords who personally work on the land should be allowed to keep land and only as much land as they need for their livelihood. The rest of the thousands of acres must be distributed free of cost among the Warlis. Without this, their economic problems cannot be solved nor their economic condition improved.

Orchards of flowers and fruits have grown in a big way in the last 10 years. *Adivasis* cannot subsist on their small holdings of land, and they do not have the equipment for orchards and irrigated farming. The lands of many such farmers were bought at 500-700 rupees per acre. Whatever the market value of land, farmers cannot live on the earnings from it. They are tempted by the lump sum. They do not think of the long run and do not try to find out the market price. They fall for the landlords' persuasive talk and the temptation of the short-term gain and sell their lands. This has added to the number of agricultural labourers. The solution to this is to make a law that *Adivasi* lands cannot be bought by non-*Adivasis*.

The other solution to improve *Adivasis*' economic conditions is to start small or medium industries in this area and to employ *Adivasis* in them. *Adivasis* are forced to work as labourers because they have neither enough land nor other occupations. But they do not find work throughout the year and seasonal work earns very low wages. Only the work of cutting grass fetches slightly better wages, but it is available for only two months in a year. The good wages here are due to the nature of the work and the *Adivasis*' unity.

Wage rates are determined every year by government officers in consultation with the traders, grass land owners, Kisan Sabha representatives, and the representatives of other parties. But grass land owners are not required by law to pay these rates and try to pay less than the rates fixed by the government officer. This leads to disputes. To prevent all this, grass land owners should be required by law to pay the fair wage rates agreed to by all parties.

There is a new practice of avoiding payment of reasonable wages. When the *Adivasis*' store of food grains is depleted, they need money. Grass land owners lend the small amounts needed for a promise to cut grass at lower wage rates. Whatever be the fair wage rate decided for the season, *Adivasis* who had borrowed are told, "I have given you money. You have to cut the grass at the agreed rate." *Adivasis* have to comply.

The other work available is farm work. The minimum wage set by law is so low that someone working at that rate must starve. The government should set rates for different kinds of farm work and non-payment of that wage should be treated as a criminal offence and suitably punished. Only then would farm labourers earn a fair wage for their work and their condition will improve.

The wage for work in the orchards was 2-4 *annas* in 1945 and is 2-2.50 rupees at most now. This wage rate is low considering the nature of the work and the labourers' needs. Only a few workers are employed throughout the year in the orchards and for the rest, this work is seasonal.

The third type of seasonal work is jungle clearing. This work lasts a worker from two to three weeks. This is very physically strenuous work. In 1947, this work was paid only 4-8 *annas.* Workers fought and struck for better wages and the rate was increased to 1.25 rupees. Prices have risen ten times in the last 20 years, but the wages have increased to less than thrice the old level. Most of this work is done by cooperative societies. The wage rates paid by societies range from 12 *annas* to 2.50 rupees. Where the workers are aware and organised, they get 2.50 rupees. Elsewhere, they have to be satisfied on 12 *annas* to a rupee. Contractors and societies avoid giving work on daily wages and prefer to pay by number of trees.

How can the *Adivasis*' economic condition improve when they have a couple of months of seasonal work at a pittance for a wage. The improvement is that, where *Adivasis* starved eight to ten months in a year, they now starve four to six months. Until *Adivasis* are given land for free and industries are started that offer jobs paying adequate salaries, the *Adivasis*' economic condition cannot improve.

Dance, hunting, and drinking are traditionally very important in *Adivasis*' lives. After the rice harvest, at the time of Diwali, the dances begin with great enthusiasm. Men and women gather in hamlets to dance. Mahalaxmi village is about 16-17 miles from

Dahanu. In the temple to the Goddess Mahalakshmi, there is a religious ritual on one Diwali day. It is like a small fair. Hundreds of young Adivasi men and women gather in the temple courtyard and dance as if in a trance. This is also a time when many men and women choose their life partners.

To buy clothes and other things for Diwali, Warlis go from their villages in the jungle to towns near the Western Railway that are 10-20 miles away, dancing all the way. The village bazaars are full of Warli crowds.

Warli women in colourful *saris*, wearing marigold and other flowers in their hair, and men dance all night to the music and the sound of anklets. It is a very beautiful sight. Men and women dance together. They form two semi-circles or crescents, one of men and one of women. The musicians stand in the centre. The men link hands and start dancing at the signal. There is nothing to see in this dance. There is no novelty in it and a spectator would find it boring. The dance is not meant to be performed for an audience but enjoyed by the dancers. It is mesmeric and the dancers do not get bored or tired.

Warli homes do not have the white collar people's deities such as Ram and Sita, Vishnu and Lakshmi, Shankar and Parvati, or Ganapati. They do not believe in these Gods. Their God is Narayan Dev. They tie peacock feathers together and anoint it God. It is called *Hirara*. They fill a basket with rice and place the God in it.

The basket is hung from the wall of a hut or a pillar. Not every *Adivasi* home has such Gods. According to tradition, the Gods are kept in one person's home. Whoever wants to worship the God takes it to his hut and returns it when done.

After the rice harvest, Warlis make a ceremonial pile of rice and offer a chicken to the Gods. From that day, they start eating newly grown rice and vegetables. Before eating pulses from a new crop, they similarly make a pile of pulses and light lamps. The village priest—bhagat—performs puja. The priests perform all ceremonies except marriages.

Nobody understands what they say. But during every ceremony, they spin around themselves as if possessed. Singing wedding songs and arranging marriages are done by one particular woman in the village. As many detailed descriptions have been written about Warli customs, I need not write at length about them here.

In 1945, when we first went to the area, Warlis had a strong belief in ghosts and spirits. There were believed to be women who prayed to and pleased the demon. It was believed that such a woman offered human sacrifices to the demon. During cholera or other epidemics, women were beaten up in the belief that they were killing people. Warlis searched for demon-worshippers and killed the suspected women.

Some of their beliefs were funny. There was believed to be a tree with black leaves, which they called the Black Enchantress. It was believed that a person who found this tree and kept a leaf with him would get money. I asked many people about it. But no one had ever seen this tree, but the myth has been handed down. Some Warlis wandered in search of this tree. Another belief is that if one holds the leaves of a particular tree in his mouth, the other person cannot think of anything to say, cannot remember anything. Some Warlis used to go to court with these leaves in their mouths.

After great efforts over the last 20 years, the practice of demon-worshipper women has disappeared in most places. Murder of a woman in this manner has stopped. Oncc party members had to be suspended for participating in such an incident. No party member took part in it again.163. But we still cannot say that this barbaric practice has ended completely. Though rare, there are still cases of killing women as Devil-worshippers.

About 75 per cent *Adivasis* have started taking medicines. They are getting vaccinated for cholera and small pox. Many are now in favour of medicines. Belief in the black enchantress and other such myths is decreasing. Belief in the priest is decreasing and with it the institution of priesthood.

"We neither believe in God nor in the Devil," we said plainly, which shocked Warlis at first, but had an effect later. Beliefs grown out of superstition and orthodoxy are disappearing slowly. The credit for this goes to party workers from the *Adivasi* community besides us. They constantly campaigned against superstitions.

Adivasis have not made much progress in the area of education. Most of the hut-like schools built after 1947 according to the Wandrekar plan have collapsed by now. Some new hut-like schools have been built while some old ones have been repaired. But schools do not run properly in this area. Teachers are unwilling to live in the jungle. They do not get newspapers, even milk for tea. They have to live in a hut or in a room partitioned off in the school building. They cannot live there with their families. There are no educational facilities for their children in the area. For all these reasons, teachers always want to go to the cities. A school may remain closed for up to a month and nobody takes notice. If a teacher is transferred to this area, it is seen as punishment. Teachers heave a sigh of relief when they are transferred out. In such conditions, what education can the schools give? There are a few ashramshalas that have benefited Warlis, but they are so few in number that they cannot bring about educational progress. The schools are so bad that students who complete the 7th standard cannot even write Marathi properly. We taught some of these children to write every day for six months and then they were able to write Marathi. Most children view schools as the means to get jobs as forester, beat guard, primary school teacher, and gramsevak or village worker. Most of the ashramshalas constantly engage in propaganda against the red flag and the Communist Party. Because of this, the public has no respect or affection for them. Only because there are no other schools, do they go to these ashramshalas. Due to all these reason and the Warlis' difficult economic condition, there has not been much progress in the field of education in the past 20 years.

The question then is what have the Warlis gained in the past 20 years? The wages increased a little and the clothes improved. The loin cloths and half-length *saris* have been replaced by half pants, pyjamas, and full-length *saris*. The new generation does not wear topknots and the women groom their hair with oil and combing. Warli homes have brass or copper kitchenware and cups and saucers. Is this the difference? Is this development? No!

The important change in Warlis is that their self-respect has been awakened. They have gained confidence from being organised and it is reflected in their behaviour. They have lost their timidity and the feeling of inferiority. They have ambitions. They have the curiosity to understand world politics. I can do something, I have the right to live as a human being—they believe this now. I have been looted and exploited—this has started to bother them. They have an urge to improve their conditions and are prepared to work hard to achieve it. Their language has also changed. The Warli who was afraid to speak a word now makes political speeches from a podium. This gives hope. The Warli who fought injustice will not fail to take the next steps. The preparation for those next steps were made during the years of the protest movement, and that is the Warlis' and our real achievement.

About the Author

Godavari Parulekar was a social activist who spent more than four decades of her life in the tribal belt of Thane, home to the Warli tribe. She belonged to an upper middle class family of Pune but, influenced by Marxist ideology, decided to dedicate her life to the social and political upliftment of the *Adivasis* who had been crushed under the dual yoke of British rule and upper caste landlords.

About the Translator

Nikhil Gavankar is a cost accountant and a certified public accountant from New Hampshire, USA, and has been a finance professional for more than 16 years. He has worked with several Indian and multinational companies and is currently working for the multinational IT company SunGard as Director - Business Development. He has an avid interest in literature, philosophy, psychology and other social sciences and the humanities, and has a Masters in Philosophy from SP College, University of Pune.